What's The Price For Your Soul?

WHAT'S THE PRICE FOR YOUR SOUL?

OLIVE G. CAMERON

authorHOUSE®

AuthorHouse™
1663 Liberty Drive
Bloomington, IN 47403
www.authorhouse.com
Phone: 1-800-839-8640

First published by AuthorHouse   11/12/2011

ISBN: 978-1-4685-0065-3 (sc)
ISBN: 978-1-4685-0063-9 (hc)
ISBN: 978-1-4685-0064-6 (ebk)

Library of Congress Control Number: 2011960383

Printed in the United States of America

CONTENTS

DEDICATION

To my heavenly Father and the Lord Jesus Christ without whom I never would have been able to come up with this title much less write an entire book. Father, I want to thank you for this opportunity that You have given me. I give You all the honor, glory, and praise for what You've done, are doing, and will do in my life. Thank You for being God and God alone. You are Lord of all glory and the Lord of my life. There is none like You and I love You with all my heart, soul, and mind. Thank You for who You are; You're so loving, good, and kind and there is no place else I'd rather be than in Your presence.

ACKNOWLEDGEMENTS

I would like to thank my Lord and savior Jesus Christ, without whom I would not be able to do this. To my children, Samuel and Sean Cameron for being so patient with me for spending so much time on this project and for being in my life as my inspiration. I would like to thank my mother for believing in me and encouraging me through rough times. I would also like to thank my grandmother for showing me true love and for praying for me since I was a child. I also want to thank those who talked about me, laughed at me, and called me crazy for doing what God said. Finally, I thank the publisher and the editors of the manuscript, Travern Beerom and Gretna Wilkinson. Thank you all for pitching in to help make this happen.

PREFACE

The purpose of this book is to let you see where you are in God, to help you change your life and get closer to God. You know that you are in relationship with God when you pray every day, not just five or ten minutes, but at least an hour per day and read your bible every day. If you're not doing this, then you do not have that relationship like you think. If you're opening your bible only when you go to church on Sundays, then you do not have a relationship with God. Everybody says they love God, but they do not want to take time out to spend with Him. However, when they are in a bind then they call on God like He was their genie to get them out of the situation. It does not work like that. You have to build a relationship with Him, and He will help you to get closer to Him because He loves you that much.

When you have a relationship with God, you will also give your tithes and offering because you love Him and want to be pleasing to Him. You will love not just your family and friends; Jesus said that people in the world love their family and friends as well, but with God you will love those that are not loveable and you will always give to the poor and needy. When you have a relationship with God, you will do what He tells you to do.

A relationship does not come easy, but you will do everything in your power and in your ability to make it work. As you grow in God, you will also fast more often in order for those things that are not like Him to be taken away from you. You will also want to do the right things to please Him. It is easier to do the wrong thing than to do the right thing. God is a loving and forgiving God but when you chose to do the right things over the wrong things, God will give you an extra blessing because He knows how difficult it was for you to choose good over your own lust and enticement.

It pleases God very much when He sees you working in the position that He has ordained for you, and when you go all out for God He will go all out for you. Always give God the things that He has asks for. He will never harm you in anyway and He always wants what's best for you. Loving God comes with knowing God and knowing God comes from spending time with Him. If you say that you love Him and do not spend time with Him then you're a liar and the truth is not in you just as you're a liar if you say you love God and not the people you see around you every day.

God is faithful to His word and whatever God says to you will come true; all you have to do is praise Him and watch things come to pass in due time. Do not be afraid if and when God starts working on you. He is changing your character to be Christ-like. He wants to be proud of you because you represent Him in every way, so He puts character inside of you for others to see that you are His and His alone.

Do not be in too much of a hurry to come out of your wilderness; wait until God takes you out. When He does, it will mean that you are ready to go to where He has ordained and destined for you to go. Love the Lord with all your heart, body, mind, soul, and spirit. He will love you back and give you things that you never thought were possible. Not just material things but spiritual things, which are by far more important.

As you get closer to God, you will find yourself being on time and being faithful in whatever you do. You will find yourself paying your tithes and offerings no matter what or how short you think you are. You will go out of your way to help those that are in need and you will give up things that displease Him. When you do, you will find that God is pleased with you and will give you the things that your heart so desires.

INTRODUCTION

Are you saved? How do you know you are saved? When you die would you go to heaven? These are questions we should ask ourselves because in Philippians 2:12 Paul states:

> *Therefore, my dear ones, as you have always obeyed [my suggestions], so now, not only [with the enthusiasm you would show] in my presence but much more because I am absent, work out (cultivate, carry out the goal, and fully complete) your own salvation with reverence and awe and trembling (self-distrust, with serious caution, tenderness of conscience, watchfulness against temptation, timidly shrinking from whatever might offend God and discredit the name of Christ).*

What is the price for your soul? What are you willing to pay for it? What would you give in exchange for your soul? Could you afford the price? Do you know that a price was paid? What is your part in this? Have you considered where you want to spend eternity? Where would it be? I'm sure you think that you are a good person, but do you know that being good cannot get you into heaven? So where will you spend eternity? Heaven, or hell, which one will it be?

These are real questions that need some real answers. Look over your life and write down what you think. Well, what did you come up with since you know now that being good will not get you into heaven? Keeping the commandments is one of the keys that would get you to heaven. Are you being realistic or are you fooling yourself? This is not a game. It's your life we're talking about, so be true to yourself. Go on; look over your life. Again, where would you spend eternity, heaven or hell?

The whole purpose of Jesus' coming was what? Well, are you pleasing in His sight? Are you doing what He commanded you to do? Is your life pleasing to Him or is He disappointed in you? So we go back to the question, are you saved? There are many ways to answer this question. Look at how many years you've been saved; are you growing spiritually? How do you know that you are? Is your life at a stand still? Why? This book will be like looking into a mirror, but instead of looking at the reflection of your face you will be looking at the reflection of your soul and how you are inside. It will also show you how you can make the changes that you need, to develop the kind of relationship you need with the Lord and with others. It will help you to see where you are in Christ, what you should and should not do, and how to get back to or higher in God.

CHAPTER 1
ARE YOU SAVED?

The first thing we need to look at is, are you saved; and how do you know that you are? I know that this is a very touchy subject for a lot of people because you're already saying with an attitude, "Yes. I'm saved and I've been saved for years." But what you do not realize is, not because you go to church every Sunday means you're saved.

Jesus stated in Matthew 7:22-23:

> *Many will say to Me in that day, Lord, Lord, have we not prophesied in Your name and drive out demons in Your name and done many mighty works in Your name. And then I will say to them openly (publicly), I never knew you; depart from Me, you who act wickedly [disregarding My commands].*

Officiously those people were churchgoers, but yet they went to hell. Remember Samuel the prophet whose words never fell to the ground; after his mother had given him back to the Lord how he ministered before Eli, but he knew not the Lord?

In 1Samuel 3: 1-7 states:

> *Now the boy Samuel ministered to the Lord before Eli. The word of the Lord was rare and precious in those days; there was no frequent or widely spread vision. At that time Eli, whose eyesight had dimmed so that he could not see, was laying down in his own place. The lamp of God had not yet gone out of the temple of the Lord, where the ark of God was, and Samuel was laying down. When the Lord called, Samuel! And he answered here I am. He ran to Eli and said; here I am, for you call me. Eli said, I did not call you; lie down again. So he went and lay down. And the Lord Called Again,*

1

Samuel! And Samuel arose and went to Eli and said, here am I; you did call me. Eli answered, I did not call, my son; lie down again. Now Samuel did not yet know the Lord, and the word of the Lord was not yet revealed to him.

Although Samuel was working and ministering to the Lord he did not know Him. The same can happen to us; we can be working in the ministry and do not know the Lord. We get so busy in serving and ministering for the Lord that we forget to spend time in getting to know Him, and we neglect spending personal time with Him, and in so doing we send our own selves to hell.

Now put aside your pride just this once and lets go through your life and make sure you would not be the one to whom Jesus would say, "depart from Me I know you not." This is important because I have seen too many people who claim to love God, spoke in tongues, yet they ended up in hell. If I ask anyone if they love God they would not say no, but yes. Do you know that the devil speak in tongues too? There are many people who speak in tongues that the enemy has placed them inside the church as a religious spirit. They can do the exact same things as Christians can do, they might even do it better. They are not easily detected. They're like twins. They look like Christians. They sound like Christians. They speak and know the word (in most cases) better than Christians. They can be very articulate. They sing and praise God as Christians do. They speak also in a different language like Christians do, (which we as Christians call speaking in tongues). They can also even be preaching the word.

It is hard to differentiate the real Christian from the religious Christian spirit. Not because you go through the motions of what is considered Christianity means that you are saved. The devil cannot and never ever will be saved and he will manipulate those into thinking that they are saved.

In Matthew 13:24-30 states:

Another parable He set forth before them, saying, the kingdom of heaven is like a man who sowed good seed in his field, but while he was sleeping, his enemy came and sowed also darnel (weeds resembling wheat) among the wheat, and went on his way. So when the plants sprouted and formed grain, the darnel (weeds) appeared also. And the servants of the owner came to him and said, sir, did you not sow good seed in your field? Then how does it have darnel shoots in it? He replied to them, an enemy has done this. The servants said to him, then do you want us to go and weed them out? But he said, no, lest in gathering the wild wheat (weeds resembling wheat), you root up the [true] wheat along with it. Let them grow together until the harvest; and at harvest time I will say to the reapers, gather the darnel first and bind it in bundles to be burned, but gather the wheat into my granary.

So you see, it is very difficult to tell the real Christian (a believer and lover of God) from the religious Christian (the ones pretending to be and those that Satan has planted). We have to let them alone until Jesus comes and He will separate. It might not be until then that you realize you might be one of them, and by that time it will be too late. How do I know that they are in hell, you ask? Well, that's because they were too mean and nasty, and meanness can never enter heaven.

I knew of a woman that went to church all the time. Everyone called her "Mother." Not only was she elderly but she was also a minister supporting the people and someone you can talk to when you're down. She gave advice and wisdom. I was once told that she spoke with the tongue of an angel. (That's speaking in a different language beautifully). It seemed that she had it all together. One day she told a friend of mine that her daughter had been working witchcraft (for those in the Islands it's obeah) on her for years and it's getting stronger.

Now, tell me, if you've been a Christian for years and speaking with such marvelous, melodious tongues; then how on earth would witchcraft get stronger in your life when Christ the Hope of Glory lives in you? It was not that the witchcraft was getting stronger; it was that her faith and beliefs in God were getting weaker. She did the motions of a Christian; but in reality, she was a Christian in religion only. When you've been in church for a very long time and you slip away from God you still end up doing what you used to do. You do not forget how to speak in tongues; nor do you forget how to get your dance on. You can fool the people of God, you can even fool yourself, but you cannot fool God.

He knows everything, what you think, what you feel, even what's in your mind and in your heart. Weeks later, the woman came home from having dinner with friends (you know how it is when people think that you're the cats' meow and the dogs' bowwow, everyone wants to spend time with you, taking you here, there and everywhere). She went to her room, took a shower like she always does before bed. Her granddaughter stated that after she went to bed she heard her crying out, "Bring ice; bring ice; I'm hot; I'm hot; bring ice." The granddaughter said she ran into the room to see what was going on and if her grandmother was okay, but when she got there, she saw her grandmother, the woman of great tongues and ministry, the woman to whom everyone went for guidance, council and support. She had folded her fist fighting something that was not there or at least could not be seen by the naked eye.

She was fighting something physically when she should have been fighting it spiritually. That is what the word of God is for. It is to be used in times of trouble, in times when our adversary, the devil is attacking us the most. We must not forget why the word of God is so vitally important; it can save your life. Speaking the right word at the right time can and will get you out of trouble and save your very soul.

THE SPIRIT WORLD

The spirit world is real, even more real than this one. It is where you will go after death and that's for eternity. In this life we may live one hundred years, maybe even one hundred and twenty; but no matter how long you live on this earth your lifetime span is still short, much shorter than that of eternity. So the spirit world is more real, for its forever.

That night the woman died. Heaven or hell, where do you think she went? Which one did she make her home? Well, according to the scriptures you die in peace when you die in the Lord. (*Absent from the body present with the Lord*). This woman had no peaceful death. She was calling for ice because she was so hot. (Do you know of a place that the bible says was hot?) Of course you do. Jesus said, "*Hell is where the fire is never quenched and the worms dieth not.*"

That means, it is a very hot place and many times especially when people are about to die, there always seems to be some kind of reaction whether it's a good reaction or a bad reaction. Normally, from these reactions you know whether or not the person has accepted Jesus as their Lord and Savior.

Many people do not want to think that their family member has died and gone to hell; but the reality is, far too many people have died and are dying without Christ. We all think that they were saved because they went to church often and acted like they were saved. We do not want to think that they have died without

Christ and are now in hell. We think maybe at the last minute that God will step in and save them, or at least they came to make piece with their Maker when no one has even offered them salvation or spoken to them regarding their Christian walk. The reason no one offered them salvation is because they thought that they already had salvation in the way in which they acted. In most cases, it's too late to wait until death's bed to surrender your life to Christ because you might not get that chance with hell's gate at your door fighting for your very soul.

Like this woman was fighting back physically instead of with the word of God, you become too busy fighting off demons and forget to call on God. Demons cannot be fought off by your fists and legs. You've got to be crazy to think that will make them go away. You can only fight them off with God's word. However, just saying them would not be enough if Jesus is not in you, for if He be not in you, then the word will not work for you. The devil knows the word too; that's how he can use it against you if you do not know it. He used it on Jesus and he will definitely use it on you.

In Ephesians 6:12 states:

> *For we are not wrestling with flesh and blood [contending only with physical opponents], but against the despotisms, against the powers, against [the master spirits who are] the world rulers of this present darkness, against the spirit forces of wickedness in the heavenly (supernatural) sphere.*

When you're fighting the enemy you must know that:

1. The devil is a spirit.
2. We must tap into our spirit, and God is the Spirit in us that we tap into.
3. We speak to the enemy through God's word.

4. We fight back by standing and facing the enemy and not turning and running.

This means you can never overcome them by physical means. You have to overcome them spiritually; and without God and His word, you are doomed.

THE ENEMY USES THE WORD

The enemy uses the word also; the only difference is that he twists it to suit his own needs in order to trip us up. The devil will always use the word to suit his needs to get you to mess your life up. The word he brings is very similar to what God says. He also tries to sound like God (so watch out). The only thing with that is; either he leaves some parts out or he adds some parts; either way, you will be fooled if you do not know the word for yourself.

Once, after I first got saved the devil told me that the archangel Gabriel was the one who fell from grace and not Lucifer. I knew my word enough to know better. You see how he tries to trick you? Yes, someone fell from grace but it was not Gabriel, it was Lucifer. He just turned it around, and if you do not know better you would take what he said at face value. If you know the word of God for yourself and Christ is in you, then you will be able to say as Jesus said, "It is written; it is written." So the devil has been here on earth for thousands of years; he knows the Bible. He's like a dinosaur—old and very dangerous. Knowing the word does not mean that God will answer him and save his soul (that's if he had one).

The same goes for us. It does not mean God will answer you when you speak His word. You can speak it all you want and that still would not get the devil off of you. Jesus has to be in you. He it is that gives you power to speak to the enemy and make him flee. Jesus is the One that resides in you, that when you speak, it is actually He speaking through you to the enemy, and that's how and why the enemy has to flee from you. Remember the seven sons of Sceva?

In Acts 19:13-16 states:

> *Then some of the traveling Jewish exorcists (men who adjure evil spirits) also undertook to call the name of the Lord Jesus over those who had evil spirits, saying, I solemnly implore and charge you by the Jesus whom Paul preaches. Seven sons of a certain Jewish chief priest named Sceva were doing this. But [one] evil spirit retorted, Jesus I know, and Paul I know about, but who are you? Then the man in whom the evil spirit dwelt leaped upon them, mastering two of them, and was so violent against them that they dashed out of that house [in fear], stripped naked and wounded.*

So you see that just speaking the word does not get you anywhere but more demons attaching themselves to you. You have to make sure that you are in relationship with God before you try to do something that you are not ready for. If you're not close to God you cannot overcome the enemy. They are different levels of demons. You have to know how strong you are in God. You have to know if you're ready to cast out demons. You cannot cast out demons unprepared. You have to be released by God.

However, some of you not only have no power, you have no Jesus. Remember, no Jesus, no power. Your words become as sounding brass and tinkling symbols. They become empty. So you go to church and you speak in tongues, but is Christ living in you? It's just you alone reading this book. Well, answer the question; be true to yourself. No one will judge you; you can only judge yourself. Do demons know who you are? Can they say about you the same as they said about Paul? Are they afraid of you? Do they dread when you awake in the mornings? Only you can answer these questions. Only you know the truth. If you would be true to yourself then this book can help you. If you would not be true to yourself then not only are you lying to yourself, but you are doing a great disservice to yourself. If you are a true believer, the devil does not only know who you are but he sure knows your name.

Too many people are dying and going to hell. We have to do something about it. We as believers must educate ourselves, make sure that we are saved, then go out there and win others for Christ. It's time to step up to the plate, quit yourselves as men and women of the Lord Jesus Christ making sure you're in the faith; and lets win the world for Christ.

The woman I spoke of earlier was a churchgoer all her life. She even prophesied to others, she said that God had told her to move from one state to another but died before she could make that move. Now, you know when God says something, it has to come to pass, and make sure you reach your destination before you die. Too many people have been making a mockery of God, trying to seem important by saying things that God did not say and causing others to fall because of it. Be aware of those people. That's why I'm very leery of those who always say, "God said." It's not time for slacking off. We have wasted too much time as the body of Christ; its time to take a stand, and it starts with you, the church.

I knew another woman who never set foot in a church, and when she died, her son told me that just before she passed away she was lying in the bed crying, "I'm falling, I'm falling." She was falling into outer darkness. She knew not the Lord and so her death experience was different. Don't get me wrong, I know that death not only comes different for everyone, but there is a difference in how one is taken into the afterlife. The woman who went to church all her life was being mocked by the enemy and was experiencing the heat of hell just before death while the woman who never went to church and had never experience God for herself was taken into the afterlife in a different way. Both, however, did not die a peaceful death that is promised to those who love the Lord.

ANOTHER CHANCE

My dear friends, it's real. We're all going to die one day. God has given us another chance to make things right. All your hatred, anger, unforgiveness, and jealousy; get rid of them because none of these things will inherit the kingdom of God. Some of you right now are saying, "These things will not keep me out of heaven." If you just said that then you are one that needs to rededicate your life to Christ.

Some might be saying, "I have only one, but I do everything else right." You can do all things right, but if you have hatred or unforgiveness in your heart you will still be left behind; it disqualifies you from heaven. Unless you get rid of it you will not enter in. The sad thing is that we believe that Jesus is God's Son that He was born of the Virgin Mary, that He died for our sins and that God raised Him upon the third day. The problem is that we never took the time to know Him. That meant that we rejected Him, and that would cost us spending eternity with our Lord and Savior.

Some of you are saying, "But that's harsh and God would not allow that to happen." You're right; He is a loving and forgiving God. Why would He not let that happen? I'll tell you why He would let that happen; God sent His one and only Son to die on a cross for you, and you rejected Him. God has given you many chances even one right now by having you read this book. If you still reject Him or still think that you have no need of repenting because you've been saved all your life, then think again. He will most certainly cast you into the lake of fire. What you are saying by rejecting Him is that you do not love Him and what He has done is or was not good enough. As merciful and as loving and as forgiving our God is, there comes a time when He says, "No more."

In Genesis 6:3 states: *Then the Lord said, My Spirit shall not forever dwell and strive with man, for he also is flesh; but his days shall yet be 120 years.*

If God keeps coming to you and you keep on ignoring, refusing and rejecting Him, then He will stop coming to you. God will give up on you. He will turn you into a reprobate mind. He will not hear when you call. You will be no longer His. He will allow the enemy to have his way with you. He gives us our lifetime to get it right and with His help we would be what He wants us to be, but you have to do your part. His part is finished. On the cross Jesus said, "*It is finished*" not, "It has to be continued."

James 4:8 states:

> *Come close to God and He will come close to you. [Recognize that you are] sinners get your soiled hands clean; [realize that you have been disloyal] wavering individuals with divided interests, and purify your hearts [of your spiritual adultery].*

Because Jesus did what He did on the cross, His part is now over and you now have to make the next move. When you make that move He will step in and help you. It's your move now.

CHAPTER 2
THE CHRISTIAN PERSON

What is a Christian in religion, and how do you know if you are a Christian? Well, a Christian is a person who accepted Jesus Christ as his or her Lord and Savior. In other words he or she belongs to Christ. These are some of the beliefs of a Christian person.

1. They believe that Jesus was born of the Virgin Mary.
2. They believe that He is the Son of God.
3. They believe that Jesus died on a cross at Calvary.
4. They believe that His blood was shed for the remission of their sins.
5. They believe that God raised Him from the dead on the third day.
6. They believe that He is seated at the right hand of God the Father.
7. They believe that He will return for them.

A Christian person also seeks God's face. They pray everyday no matter what is going on in their life. They praise God through the good times, and they praise God through the bad times. They fast often in order to overcome situations that seem to have a strong hold. They put God first in all that they do. They spend quality time with Him, because He is their Father and because they love Him too. They read the bible everyday come what may. They learn as much as they can about Him, and they do this through His word. Spending time and memorizing scriptures is the only way to know what God say, especially about a situation they may be going through.

In Acts 11:26 states:

> *And when He found him, he brought Him back to Antioch. For a whole year they assembled together with and were guests*

of the church and instructed a large number of people; and in Antioch the disciples were first called Christians.

This was how the name Christian came about. They seek to spend that quality time with Him everyday. In other words, they have a relationship with God. They also go to church as often as they can. They go to church because they need to fellowship with their brothers and sisters in Christ. They go to hear what thus said the Lord for that situation they may have had to face that week. They also need to go to worship God in unity and in public. They also go to strengthen each other in the Lord, and they are faithful in attendance.

In Hebrews 10:25 Paul said:

Not forsaking or neglecting to assemble together [as believers], as is the habit of some people, but admonishing (warning, urging, and encouraging) one another, and all the more faithfully as you see the day approaching.

Christians feels lost if they do not spend personal time with God. They do whatever is necessary to make sure that they get the time they need to spend with Him because it is vital for their existence. They are not mean and nasty to others. Christians also help others and they do not talk about them or 'put them down' no matter what. They are always on the look out everyday to see whom they can help. They are always stretching their hands to the needy and helpless. They walk with God, not in front of Him or behind Him, but with Him. They are a pattern for Christ because they represent Him in everyway. These are the people who care, who would go out of their way to help those that are in need. They would not think twice to do what God wants them to do. They are out to please God in every way and in everything that they do.

1 Peter 3:8-11 states:

Finally, all [of you] should be of one and the same mind (united in spirit), sympathizing [with one another], loving [each other] as brethren [of one household]. Compassionate and courteous (tenderhearted and humble). Never return evil for evil or insult for insult (scolding, tongue-lashing, berating), but on the contrary blessing [praying for their welfare, happiness, and protection, and truly pitying and loving them]. For know that to this you have been called, that you may yourself inherit a blessing [from God-that you may obtain a blessing as heirs, bringing welfare and happiness and protection]. For let him who wants to enjoy life and see good days [good-whether apparent or not] keep his tongue free from evil and his lips from guile (treachery, deceit). Let him turn away from wickedness and shun it, and let him do right. Let him search for peace (harmony; undisturbedness from fears, agitating passions, and moral conflicts) and seek it eagerly. [Do not merely desire peaceful relations with God, with your fellowmen, and with yourself, but pursue, go after them].

When you're a Christian, you automatically get many benefits from the Lord. Other than the fact that He will love you and care for you, He will also do more for you than you could imagine. These are just some of the benefits for a believer.

1. You could approach God directly.
2. You will find help in your daily problems and in times of trouble.
3. You will be empowered to serve God.
4. You will become part of God's plan to build the body of Christ.
5. You become one with the body of Christ all across the nation (becoming brothers and sisters).

6. You also partake in being a part of reconciling God and man.
7. You will get to rule and reign with Him.

Christian people are those who have the Holy Spirit living inside and residing in them. By sincerely trusting and acknowledging Jesus as Lord and Savior, He then comes into your life; not always feeling anything supernatural, but once you are sincere He will automatically come in.

THE RELIGIOUS PERSON

Religious people are those who go to church every Sunday and go through the motions of raising their hands and dancing to the music and enjoying the service like it was just entertainment and leave the same way they came. No change. They also believe the same things as a real Christian does. They just do not practice living the God kind of life in their everyday lives. They do not have the relationship with God; they have the relationship with the church. They think that if they go to church, they are saved.

The devil goes to church too; is he saved? Of course not, how can he be? These people are ready to curse you out in the parking lot and fight you for a seat. They call themselves Christian because that would be the name of the religion. Such like a Muslim who is a follower of Islam. If I were to ask them what religion they are of, they would say, "I am a Muslim." Well, it's the same way with Christianity; they say that they are Christians because they believe in Jesus Christ, but their behavior is not that of a believer. They are not in tune with God. They are too carnally-minded. They still do the same things they did before they were saved. They will 'go off' on you in a minute. They are not spiritually-minded. They walk behind God. They do not have a relationship with Him.

If someone says she is a Christian, it could simply mean she is a Christian by religion only and does not have a relationship with the Lord Jesus. These people go to church on Sunday, but Monday through Saturday they live any way they want. They do not pray or read the Bible. They curse if someone steps on their toes, cuts someone off while driving, go places they should not go, smoke pot or crack and other like manner. Don't get me wrong; when you come to Jesus it's a process of overcoming the things that you are used to; but if you've been saved for years you should have gotten over those things by now if you had continued in prayer and fasting. If you are still doing these things, it simply means that you in and of yourself do not want to change. You think that maybe these things cannot possibly keep you out of heaven, you may not be ready to serve the Lord or you may not want to give up what you are doing for Him so you do nothing about it. Remember, it takes you to want to change. He will give you the grace to overcome your obstacles, if you are willing and ready to change.

When I was about twenty or so I called myself a Christian because I went to church every time the church doors were opened. At church was the only time I opened my bible. I also used to pray just before I fell asleep. You could not tell me that I was not saved; I knew that I would have made it to heaven if Jesus came. I'm so glad He did not come before because I most surely would have gone to hell because I was still mean and nasty to people. I had no relationship with God, yet I thought that I would have made it into heaven. I was not keeping His commandments and I most certainly did not spend quality time with Him. I was a person doing all the religious acts and thinking that I loved God, but I never really had Him in my heart as much as I thought I did. Most of us go through the same thing and are still there today, the good news is that you can change things around and get out of that religious mind set and turn it into a relationship with God because that is His desire for us.

A CHRISTIAN IN RELIGION

Now, a Christian in religion believes in Jesus and all that He came to earth to do. These people come to church, raise their hands, sing and dance, and it looks like they have the Holy Ghost. They act like they have the Holy Ghost, but they do not. Their hearts are far from God. Their characters do not match what they claim to be and they definitely do not bear fruit. They think they are better than anyone else. They turn up their noses at the less fortunate, and they think God loves them more than anybody else because He may have spoken to them a time or two. They also try to please man rather than God. They have not grown at all and it seems that they do not wish to grow. They are satisfied with where they are and who they have become and in most cases making other people's lives miserable because they are so mean.

The devil has lied to them telling them they are saved even if they do wrong and they do not need to repent because it was okay to do that which was wrong. They are not even sure what is right from what is wrong anymore. I guarantee you one thing; if you are having doubts about your walk with God and you are questioning whether you're saved or not, it's not because the devil is asking you, it's because the Holy Spirit is convicting you.

Isaiah 29:13 states:

> *And the Lord said, forasmuch as this people draw near Me with their mouth and honor Me with their lips but remove their hearts and minds far from Me and their fear and reverence for Me are a commandment of men that is learned by repetition [without any thought as to the meaning].*

In other words, God is not pleased with them. They give God lip service, their hearts are far from God; they get nothing out of the preaching; they are too overly spiritual; they walk ahead of God; and they feel they know everything.

Now, how do you know that you are a Christian in religion? If you would be honest with yourself, you would take a pen and a pad or use the note pages at the back of this book and start examining yourself. You do want to be the way God wants you to be, right? So get yourself together and make your life the way that God wants.

1. Check to see if you're in the faith.
2. Write down how many years you've been saved.
3. Ask yourself, have you grown from year to year or are you still in the same place where you first got saved?
4. Check your heart and see how many times you've been mean or short with someone, even this week.
5. Ask yourself, what is the purpose of my going to church?

When you ask yourself question number five, answer it. What did you come up with? If it is any other reason than to stay saved, to fellowship with believers, to hear what thus saith the Lord for your life, to worship God openly and publicly and to grow spiritually, then you are going for other reasons which will not bring about change in your life. When you go to church do you go because you feel you have to or because you want to? If you are going to find a husband or a wife, to see what others are wearing, to say that you've made your quota, to see the pastor, to show off your new clothes, you are then going for the wrong reasons. It is not enough to act religious. We must be sincere. Now, if you are going to church for the wrong reasons, ask God to forgive you, repent (it simply means to change your ways, your mind, and to change direction). We want to get your life right with God; it is a matter of life and death.

THE IMPORTANCE OF CHURCH

Going to church is important. Some people feel that they do not need to go to church. They feel they have enough God in them that they do not think it necessary. Sometimes we go through so much in a weak and we need to hear an encouraging word. We need to hear a word from the Lord. What is God saying regarding this situation that I'm in? Sometimes you might have heard God say something to you and when you went to church the Lord used the preacher or someone else to say the same things He had spoken to you about; and there, thus giving you a confirmation.

God will always meet you at your point of need. He will always give you a confirmation on what He has said. It can come from anyone. God does not have to do it the same way today as He did it yesterday. It can come from the preacher, and it does not have to be the regular pastor of that church. It can come from the person sitting right next to you. It can come from the person opening up in prayer. It can come from the person who is leading the praise and worship. It can come from the person who reads the scripture for the day. It can come from the person making the announcements. God can send His word through anyone He chooses, but you bet it's coming. People who go to church just to say, "I went to church today, I've made my quota" are there just to take up a seat. The word comes forth and it goes through one ear and out the next. Jesus spoke about this in the parable of the sower.

Matthew 13:3-8 states:

> *And He told them many things in parables (stories by the way of illustration and comparison), saying, a sower went out to sow. And as he sowed, some seeds fell by the roadside and the birds came and ate them up. Other seeds fell on rocky ground, where they had not much soil; and at once they sprang up,*

because they had no dept of soil. But when the sun rose, they were scorched, and because they had no root, they dried up and withered away. Other seeds fell among thorns, and the thorns grew up and chocked them out. Other seeds fell on good soil, and yielded grain-some a hundred times as much as was sown, some sixty times as much, and some thirty.

We need to be careful; we could end up getting stuck in a situation of thinking that where we are in life is just good enough, and go through the same cycle year after year after year. This mentality is mediocrity, and we need to come out from that. We should want more, but you have to want to want more. Then and only then can we see the truth of this slump that we have put ourselves in. This is the answer to the parable.

Matthew 13:18-23 states:

Listen then to the [meaning of the] parable of the sewer. While anyone is hearing the word of the kingdom and does not grasp and comprehend it, the evil one comes and snatches away what was sown in his heart. This is what was sown along the roadside. As for what was sown on thin (rocky) soil, this is he who hears the word and at once welcomes and accepts it with joy; yet it has no real root in him, but is temporary (inconstant, lasts but a little while); and when affliction or trouble or persecution comes on account of the word, at once he is caused to stumble [he is repelled and begins to distrust and desert Him whom he ought to trust and obey] and he falls away. As for what was sown among thorns, this is he who hears the word, but the cares of the world and the pleasure and delight and glamour and deceitfulness of riches choke and suffocate the word, and it yields no fruit. As for what was sown on good soil, this is he who hears the word and grasps and comprehends it; he indeed bears fruit and yields in one case a hundred times as much as was sown, in another sixty times as much, and in another thirty.

Which one are you? Be honest with yourself. It's just you and God. He knows you. He loves you and wants the best for you. Never think that God does not care about you, (that's a lie from the pit of hell) a lie from the devil. Remember, he is the father of lies. Recognizing your problems is the first step to becoming what God will have you be. God wants to use you, to bring you to the forefront, to bring you into a place of blessings. He cannot do that unless He works out in you the things that are not like Him. Let Him have free reign in your life.

There are things in your life that you will not let go of that easily, and there are things that you will let go of very easily. All in all you will hurt. You will have some discomfort, but it's holiness or hell. They no longer preach holiness or hell in the pulpits today. There are a lot of materialistic things and not enough Jesus, how to stay saved, and that He's coming back soon. So we start looking at and for material things and when it does not happen, our faith gets weak; we get frustrated and then come to church just to come. You feel like it's the same things being said and nothing applies to you because the preacher said you were going to be blessed and you were not. So you have every negative thought, and now you're just doing your part, just coming, but without any expectation and you do this Sunday after Sunday. Your prayer life then starts diminishing; then the next thing you know, you have backslidden and don't even know it.

A PERSONAL RELATIONSHIP

When you come to church and hear holiness or hell, or if you're constantly hearing "Jesus loves you" and you never get tired of hearing about the cross and what Jesus has done for you and how

God wants to transform you into Christ likeness, and that to be like Him hurts, and that you have to go without things at times, there will be more people who would develop a relationship with God for the right reasons. They will look for more spiritual things from God than material things. Material things cannot come unless or until you build your own personal relationship with God. You have to take the time to do so, it doesn't come overnight and without you doing something. When you truly want God and the things of God more than anything else, that's because you have built a love relationship with Him.

It takes time to get there. Just mentioning it is not good enough; it has to come from the heart. You can fool man, but you cannot fool God. He knows all things. Take the time to know Him. If you take the time to know God then things become an added benefit. The house becomes an added benefit. The car becomes an added benefit. The husband or wife becomes an added benefit. Abundant life becomes an added benefit. When you get a relationship with God and you're not thinking of only material things, God will eventually give you these things after you've suffered a while.

Matthew 6:33 Jesus states: *But seek (aim at and strive after) first of all His Kingdom and His righteousness (His way of doing and being right), and then all these things taken together will be given you besides.*

When you seek God with all your heart, He will be fond of you. You will also gain the things of God: knowledge, wisdom, understanding, and insight. You will gain the anointing of God. You will gain the spiritual aspects of God: the word of wisdom, discerning of spirits, faith, diverse kinds of tongues, and interpretation of tongues. You will gain the love and favor of God. You will gain all the spiritual gifts: the gift of healing, the gift of prophecy, the gift of teaching, and the gift of miracles. You will also gain power with and in God.

Material things will never come unless you make God your number one priority. They may come, but they will not last. All these things frustrate Christians because they are not aware of the truth. You may have heard, "Come to God and all things will get better, you will get a house, you will get a car, you will get a man, you will get a woman, you will get your heart's desire." Although it is not false advertising, it's just not the whole truth. What they do not or did not tell you is that in order for you to get these things, you must first go through some things before God releases any of these things to you. It may also be some horrendous things because He wants you to first build that relationship with Him. He wants you to be close to Him. Because of our carnal nature, we of course want these things and expect them immediately. Then because it does not happen, we fall back and continue our lives as if we were not saved and God has offended us. That's maybe where you are today, but I speak life to you. Loving God takes time. Spending time with God causes you to love Him. Not only love Him but also trust Him. Make Him the God of the Bible, not the God of what man says. Know Him for yourself. Know the truth about Him, and you will only know that by spending quality time with Him.

CHAPTER 3
TIME IN PRAYER

Are you spending time in prayer? I do not mean any time you feel like it. I mean are you setting aside a specific time of the day every day to spend with the Lord, where it's just you and Him? No interruptions? I know a lot of you work and have children, but I guarantee you that if you put aside some time everyday to spend with the Father, your life would change for the better. If you can spend at least two hours a day praying, singing, praising, and worshiping Him nonstop, you will build a strong relationship with Him.

I know some of you are saying, two hours? That's a long time. Well, let me ask you this, how many hours do you watch TV, or talk on the phone? Or how long do you spend on the computer? I can bet it's longer than two hours. A relationship does not happen overnight; it takes time and plenty of it. It's like when you first fell in love. You wanted to see the person every day and talk to him for hours at a time although you just saw him a minute ago. It's like you do not want to let him go, so you pick up the phone just to hear him again. Why? It's because you're in love. Well, if you spend that kind of time with God, He will make it worth your while. He will bring everything that's yours all in due time when you give Him some of your time. My time is precious to me and I hardly spend time with people because they like to waste your time and you cannot get any of it back, so I spend my time with the Father knowing that I will be productive no matter how much time I spend with Him.

The more time I spend with Him the less I have to do. He redeems the time to you and cause what would have taken an hour to do takes you only ten minutes. God works like that. You just have to trust Him and make the time for Him. I have heard people say it's not the quantity of time you spend with the Lord it's the quality of time. This is true only when you have spent quantity time with Him, then it becomes quality time.

When you first accepted Christ and began praying for example; it may have taken an hour before He shows up (that is before He manifests His presence to you where you actually feel Him). As the weeks go on, if you're faithful in your prayer everyday (and I might add that it is very important to spend the same time with the Lord to show your faithfulness); now instead of an hour before He shows up; it is now 45 minutes. As the weeks go on, instead of 45 minutes before He shows up, it is then 30 minutes; and that's how it becomes quality and not quantity. However, it takes time, days, weeks, months and yes, even years, while all along you are being consistent and faithful in what you do. If you are faithful to Him, He will be faithful to you. You may say, "I do not have that kind of time." Then start with fifteen minutes, but make sure you ask Him for more time with Him and He will give it to you.

When I first got saved, I used to pray before I went to work. Every day I would have to go to work either for 8am or 10am. I would always pray before I went, and every time I was getting into my prayer I had to leave for work. I would say to the Lord, "I'm sorry but I have to go, I do not want to but I have to go to work." After one month of that the Lord was fed up with me having to leave in the middle of Him loving on me, and He told me to quit my job. When I did, I was able to pray for hours at a time. Now God does not work that way with everyone, but God will grant you the time if you ask it of Him as long as it's to spend it with Him and not for something else.

Please try to be faithful with whatever time you give Him. If you will be faithful every day with your time given to Him, then watch God open the door and grant you even more time with Him. He wants time with you more than you want with Him. He loves you so much that He will give you the time if your heart so desires it.

If you say you love God and do not want to spend time in prayer then something is wrong with that picture. If you truly love God, you will want to spend as much time as possible with Him. It will become a pleasure spending time with Him and not a chore. That's how you know that you truly love Him. You have to take the time to build that relationship; it just doesn't happen. You first have to want to spend time with Him. You have to take the time out to spend with Him. You have to put aside the time that you want to spend with Him. You have to be consistent with the time you have given to Him. You have to be willing and prepared to spend more time than you have originally planned. The reason you might spend more time is because His presence will be all over you that will cause you not to be able to move. It will cause you to just lie there until it leaves you, which could be hours. Many days I had to lie in my prayer closet until God's presence leave. It was only then I got the strength to move.

We all want things to happen overnight but it does not work that way. Yes, God could do just that; but if He does it, would you appreciate it? Or would you take it for granted? It all takes time because it took us years to be who we were before we got saved. So it will take time to change us and shape us into Christlikeness. Don't forget, our sinful nature does not want to give up the things we like doing before we got saved, so it's a constant battle between the flesh (our sinful nature) and our spirit (who we really are). We have to realize that this Christian walk is not easy; however, it is easier than living in sin.

WHO ARE YOU YOKED WITH?

There is one that you will have to choose; who it is that you want to be with? The decision you make will determine your outcome whether good or bad.

Matthew 11:28-30 Jesus states:

> *Come to Me, all you who labor and are heavy-laden and overburdened, and I will cause you to rest. [I will ease and relieve and refresh your souls.] Take my yoke upon you and learn of me, for I am gentle (meek) and humble (lowly) in heart, and you will find rest (relief and ease and refreshment and recreation and blessed quiet) for your souls. For My yoke is wholesome (useful, good-not harsh, hard, sharp, or pressing, but comfortable, gracious, and pleasant), and My burden is light and easy to be borne.*

In other words, no matter which side you are on, there will be a yoke around your neck. Whom would you prefer to be yoked with, the yoke of Jesus or the yoke of the devil? Which one is, or would be easier? The devil's yoke keeps you in bondage to sin and death and it takes a toll on you causing you shame, sickness, diseases, hardship, feebleness, hell and damnation, guilt, emptiness, pain and so much more. The devil offers you the world of things that only last for a season and then comes the aftereffect. There are just too many to name them all, but the yoke of Jesus is light, burden free. Free from death, hell, and the grave. He gives you peace in the midst of a storm. He brings contentment and satisfies your every need. He makes ways out of nowhere. He is our provider. He is everything we need and so much more. He will never leave you or forsake you. He will always be right there to give you a helping hand. He makes you not only look better but feel better as well. He gives eternal life. He's a doctor in our sick beds. He's our lawyer and judge in the courtroom. He's our present help in times of trouble.

There is no comparison on which one is the best one. Jesus said it Himself, that His is the far better one to be yoked up with. God helps us; He makes it easy for us to transition from our sinful selves into our spiritual selves. It would not be easy. Once the devil realizes that he has lost you, he will come after you with full force. When this happens to you, don't you be alarmed and don't you give in because that's what he wants you to do. He wants you to say God does not love you, that God will never do what He said, that things are too hard to handle, that God had forsaken you, that you will never come out of the situation you're in, that your life is not worth living and you want to die. The devil will make you think this is too hard and you want out, but the devil is a liar. Just hold your ground and run quickly to God in prayer and the devil will have to flee from you. The key is not to listen to what he has to say but to listen to what God says. The devil will never leave you alone. It will feel like everything bad is happening all at once, and it does not seem to cease. Just remember that God would not put more on you than you can bear. If it keeps coming then it simply means that you are stronger than you think. God is right there beside you. He did not leave you when you are going through. It just means you cannot trace Him at the present time, but He is still right there. Joshua 1:5 God says, *No man shall be able to stand before you all the days of your life. As I was with Moses, so I will be with you; I will not fail you or forsake you.*

Look at all the things that you are going through and have gone through, and you are still standing. This just simply means you are not only stronger than you think, but God is definitely with you. How else can you handle all that you've been through had it not been for the Lord that is and was on your side? In Hebrews, the Lord says we must be satisfied in our present situation. Do not complain. Just ride it out and know that He will not fail you.

Hebrews 13:5 states:

> *Let your character or moral disposition be free from love of money [including greed, avarice, lust, and craving for earthly possessions] and be satisfied with your present [circumstances and with what you have]; for He (God) Himself has said, I*

will not in any way fail you nor give you up nor leave you without support. [I will] not, [I will] not, [I will] not in any degree leave you helpless nor forsake nor let [you] down! [Assuredly not.]

The devil will throw many obstacles your way and if you are not strong enough, or if you are a person who gives up too easily, then you will buckle. Like a lot of people who buckle under pressure, that's how some people remain baby Christians even though they have been saved for 20 years. Remember your struggles and your battles only come to make you strong, not to break you down but to build you up.

WHY DID YOU STOP PRAYING?

What happened that caused you to stop praying? Was it because you felt that God was not coming through fast enough and cause you to stop believing that He was not going to come through for you? Remember that God did not leave you; you left Him all on your own. Why? Was it because you gave Him a time and He did not come through in your alluded time? You cannot put God on your timetable and expect Him to jump. When you make your request known to God just praise Him, and He will bring it about in due season, (that is when you are ready to handle it). Do not be impatient with God and give up. God will bring what He has promised to pass.

Questions to ask yourself before you make a move.

1. Did God say it or did you say it?
2. Did you get a conformation on what you thought God said?
3. Did you inquire of God to what you thought He had said?

4. Did you get the witnessing in your spirit when one of God's servants spoke to you on the behalf of God?

People try doing things on their own when they think God is taking too long. Don't try to help God as Sarah did and give her husband to her maid, because she thought He (God) was not going to do what He had promise through her, but through someone else. She made a mess of things, then turn to her husband (Abraham) and said, "My wrong be upon thee." Whenever we try to help God out, we always make a mess of things. Then God has to come in and clean the mess up.

1. He did that by telling Abraham to send the child away.
2. He did that by telling Abimelech that He would kill him if he touched Sarah (Abraham's wife).
3. He had Moses kill hundreds of people that worshiped the golden calf that Aaron made so it would not contaminate the others.
4. He did that by allowing the ground to open up swallowing the people that touch the accursed thing just to keep the plague from affecting the others.
5. He also did the same with David; God had to kill the child that David and Bathsheba had out of wedlock.

God had to clean up a lot of our messes. He's a faithful God, even when we are not faithful. When we cannot wait for what God has for us we end up blaming God for all the trouble we put ourselves in. I believe the hardest thing (well at least for me) is patience. You have to be willing to wait in order to get what you want or even be willing to be without it. Sometimes, because of lack of patience, we end up with less than God's best. Ask God to give you patience and be willing to wait it out. It will come to pass when you least expect. I know just how hard it is. Getting your blessing though too soon although it's the right one, but not the right time can trip you up. If it's not God's timing it would be more of a curse than a blessing. So don't complain if God is taking longer than usual; it's just that He's preparing you to receive your gift so it can be a blessing instead of a course. Remember there's a time for everything. Don't be in too much of a rush. Let God do His job and everything will work out just fine because He knows you better than you know you. He knows what is best for you. His plan for you is to give you an expected end. In other words, He will give you His best if you will just wait, but while you wait, stay in His face, spend time with Him, wake up early every morning and worship Him. Show Him how much you love and trust Him. Show Him that you know He knows best and you trust His process. Show Him that you are willing to do whatever it takes even if it means being without the very thing you want. Show Him that you are willing to spend not only time with Him, but you are willing to give Him anything no matter the cost. God wants to see that you are willing to be with Him more than that thing you want. He wants you to want Him more and He will make you wait until you want Him more.

DO NOT GIVE GOD SOMETHING THAT COSTS YOU NOTHING?

Do not ever give God something that costs you nothing. You're probably wondering what does that mean. You may say how can I give away something that I love and want myself? It's simple, do not give God the things you do not want, give Him something that means the most to you. For example, your prayer time, do not pray after you have finished your day and you have nothing else to do. You get up earlier, before you are required to, and spend time with Him first before starting your day. The anytime prayer is something that cost you nothing while the earlier time in prayer cost you something. No matter how tired you are, still get up. That's giving God something that cost you. Well, what did it cost you? It cost you your sleep. When you give God something that costs you nothing it does not move Him, but when you give

Him something that costs you, it compels God to come and see about you. When you give to God:

1. Is it your best you're giving to Him?
2. Is it something that you do not want that you're giving to Him?
3. Is it something that you want that you're giving to Him?
4. Is it something that God will accept?
5. Is it something that will move God to come see about you?
6. Is it something that hurts you to give to Him?

When I first got saved I went out with my ex-boyfriend because he wanted to spend some time with me. On our way back from shopping, he asked me to go to Nassau Paradise Island just to spend a few days, just him and I. We had spoken about going before I had gotten saved but we never went. So he took this time knowing how much I wanted to go, even offering me my own room. I was so torn between going with him and my walk with God. If I go I would simply repent and God would forgive me. I looked at him and turned my face, my heart burning wanting to go so badly. The decision I had to make would change things in my life knowing that if and when I go we definitely would not be staying in separate rooms. I turned and looked at him again and said, "I cannot go. I'm a Christian now and I'm not allowed." I went home that day straight into my prayer closet and cried myself to sleep. I was hurt because I wanted to go so badly. I woke up to a gentle rock and went right back to sleep. God had come to see about me.

He it was that was rocking me, because I had chosen Him over what I really wanted. That was the first time I had such an experience and knew that if I chose God over the things that I want and desire, He would always come and see about me. It compelled God to come see about me. He came and comforted me not just because I was hurting so much, but also because I had chosen Him. It was easy to have gone and then ask Him to forgive me but it pleased Him so much because it was harder to choose not to go. It also showed my love for Him and He came to comfort me telling me thanks for choosing Him over me. When you're giving to God, always make sure that you would do what you want to be done to you.

1. Always give God your best and not just a part.
2. Make sure it's something you want yourself and that it's not lame and not worthy of who He is before giving it to Him.
3. Make sure it hurts you to give it and you're not giving halfheartedly.
4. Make sure God is pleased with what you're giving.
5. Make sure you choose Him over what you really want.

By making sure of these things, you will be blessed by God knowing that because you gave Him something that meant something to you, He will come and see about you. Do not be selfish and give knowing that what you're giving does not bother you or that you just do not care.

God does not tell us to do something that is not beneficial to us. It may be something you love that's why God says to give it away. You should never give something away that you do not like only. You get no blessing in that way. God will always tell you to give away what you like; it's a form of obedience and to see how much God means to you. We just cannot see it at the moment but as you grow in God you will want to make haste and do what He says, because soon enough, and because of your obedience, a blessing will come your way.

2 Corinthians 5:7 states:

> *For we walk by faith [we regulate our lives and conduct ourselves by our convection or belief respecting man's relationship to God and divine things, with trust and holy fervor, thus we walk] not by sight or appearance.*

You're looking at what you're giving instead of what you're getting back. Just give without even expecting anything in return. Look ahead and beyond your natural sight. See what God is really saying to you when He asks you to do these things. Do not think that God is telling you to give your things away just because He does not want you to have them. He's doing it in order for you to make room for what He is about to do in your life. So you will never grow any further than your last obedience.

God does not give us just anything. He gives us His best always and we should try our best to give Him our best always. You should love and respect and have reverential fear for Him and when you do you will want to give Him your best.

2 Samuel 24:21-24 states:

> *Araunah said, why has my lord the king come to his servant? And David said, to buy the threshing floor from you, to build there an alter to the Lord that the plague may be stayed from the people. And Araunah said to David, let my lord the king take and offer up what seems good to him. Behold here are oxen for burnt sacrifice, and threshing instruments and the yokes of the oxen for wood. All this, O king, Araunah gives to the king. And Araunah said to the king, the Lord your God accepts you. But King David said to Araunah, no, but I will buy it of you for a price. I will not offer burnt offerings to the Lord my God of that which cost me nothing. So David bought the threshing floor and the oxen for fifty shekels of silver.*

The plague was stayed and there were no more deaths. It moves God to respond to you. When you first meet someone that you're interested in; you go all out for them and he/she cannot even come close to treating you as good as God can. So if you can do it for that person, you sure can do it for God. Why not go all out for the One who created you and loves you so much more than that individual ever could. When you go all out for God, God will go all out for you. He will love you through that person like you want to be loved and your relationship would be heaven on earth. So give God the one thing He wants, give Him you.

CHAPTER 4
LOSS OF DOMINION

The following chapters pertain to the person who is a non-Christian, and will explain the basics of who Christ is and what He's done for you and why you should give Him your life. I will break it down to the simplest form so you can understand. Those of you who are already Christians may also need to get back to the basics and remember what Jesus has done for you and the way you were when you first got saved.

I want to start out by saying that God loves you so much that He made me take the time out to write this book, especially the next few chapters just for you. No matter what your situation may be, just remember that God loves you just as you are and He will meet you where you are, but the good news is that He will not leave you where you are.

In the New Testament, Matthew, Mark, Luke, and John explain the reasons for Jesus being here and what He did while He was here on earth. In order for you to understand the fullness of it, we must journey back to the beginning. Genesis, which is in the Old Testament, the very first book of the Bible, God said in chapter 1verse 26

> Let us [Father, Son and Holy Spirit] <u>make mankind in our image, after Our likeness,</u> (this meant that the man God made looked like God Himself) *and let them have complete authority over the fish of the sea, the birds of the air, the [tame] beast, and over all of the earth, and over everything that creeps upon the earth.*

Now the word dominion means supreme power, ruler over everything that was given to us by God Himself. We were to rule on earth and not be afraid of anything, such as lions, tigers, bears or even snakes (which most people are afraid of and hate till today). Since then we have lost dominion, ruler ship over the earth. How did we lose dominion?

In verse 27 states: *So God created man in His own image, in the image and likeness of God He created him; male and female He created them.*

Now, the word image is the same as look alike. A person or a thing that looks very similar to another. So the man looked like or very similar to God. In verse 28 God reiterated (that means, to say something again or to repeat what was already spoken or said).

And God blessed them and said to them, be fruitful, multiply, and fill the earth, and subdue it [using all its vast resources in the service of God and man]; and have <u>dominion</u> over the fish of the sea, the birds of the air, and over every living creature that moves upon the earth.

God had every intention of having the earth full of people, animals and things.

1. God gave man dominion.
    a. Be in charge.
    b. Rule over everything.
2. God told them to be fruitful and multiply.
3. God told them that they should subdue the earth.

God made us higher than any of the creatures that He made on earth. We were made to be the Supreme Being made in His likeness and in His image. Everything else that God made were to reverence us, they were to respect us, they were to obey us and they were to befriended us. This is what should have happened but instead we are afraid of what should have been in fear of us.

God wanted us to be all we could be and we gave it up to be something that we are not and we are still doing that until this day. Not what God intended and we are trying to get things back through Jesus Christ to overcome our fears and set things right.

GOD CONFIRMS HIS WORDS

God always say something at least twice that it may be establish on earth.

In 2corinthians 13:1 states: *This is the third time I am coming to you. In the mouth of two or three witnesses shall every word be established? (KJV)*

This simply means that on two or three different times God will say something to you and confirms His word, so you will know that it was God in the first place sending you His word. God will always confirms His word, so when you hear a word from God and you hear it again from someone else or even the same person who spoke it before, now speaking it at a different day or time, it becomes established, now all you have to do is hold on to it and watch it come to pass.

These are things that will happen when and if God speaks to you:

1. God will always send someone to speak His word.
2. The Holy Spirit witness to your spirit.
3. Hearing the word two or three times it becomes established.
4. God will always confirm His word.
5. You speak back the word.
6. It will not return to God void.

Gods' word will always come true no matter how long things may take. He promised never to let His words return to Him without them first accomplishing what He sent them out to do, and that you can count on. If the word you think God said does not come through, it is simply because He did not send, speak, or say it.

THE DECEPTION OF EVE

Chapter 3 of Genesis is where the fall of man happened and where we lost dominion. Here is how.

Genesis 3:1 states:

> *Now the serpent was more subtle and crafty* (which also means cunning and clever) *than any living creature of the field, which the Lord God had made. And he [satan] said to the woman, can it really be that God has said, You shall not eat from every tree in the garden?*

Satan is an enemy of God and if he is an enemy of God that means he is an enemy of man (that is you and me). He, Satan spoke to the woman through the serpent.

1. The serpent was more cunning that's why Satan used it.
2. Satan in the serpent approached the woman.
3. Satan changes the words around that God spoke.
4. Satan deceived the woman.
5. The woman did what Satan wanted.

When you stop to listen to the enemy he will trick you in every way. Back in Genesis chapter 2 after God had created the man and placed him in the garden, God told him that he could eat of every fruit tree except one.

In Genesis 16-17 States:

And the Lord God commanded the man, saying, you may freely eat of every tree in the garden; but of the tree of the knowledge of good and evil and blessing and calamity you shall not eat, for in the day that you eat of it you shall surely die.

God warned them of what would happen if they eat the fruit. The enemy knew what would happen if they ate the fruit and he entice the woman to go against what God said.

NOT GOOD FOR MAN TO BE ALONE

So God told the man to eat of every tree except this particular one and in chapter 3 we see the enemy going to the woman, why? It's because she was not there when God said not to eat of it. Only Adam, which God had named him?

In Genesis 2:18 states: *Now the Lord God said, it is not good (sufficient, satisfactory) that the man should be alone; I will make him a helper meet (suitable, adapted, complimentary) for him.*

God wanted Adam to have a woman of his equal and who is compatible to him. That was how the woman came about. God did not want the man to be alone. The man was lonely because he saw that every living thing had a male and a female except him and his inner self wanted another like himself to be his companion. God did not want the man to be alone.

1. God saw the need that the man would have for the woman.
2. God saw that the man would be unhappy being by himself.

3. God wanted the man to have someone on his level.
4. God wanted the man to have someone to share things with.

Genesis 2:21-22 states:

> *And the Lord God caused a deep sleep to fall upon Adam; and while he slept, He took of his ribs or a part of his side and close up the [place with] flesh. And the rib or part of the side, which the Lord God had taken from the man, He built up and made into a woman, and He brought her to the man.*

So God did something the man did not expect and put him to sleep. When the man woke up there was a surprise waiting for him. He was not only very surprised; he was also very pleased to have seen this beautiful person looking him in the face.

God made the woman to perfectly suit Adam and Adam alone. He knew exactly what Adam needed in a woman to off set his other side (what was missing that only the woman can bring to him) and provided it for him without him even asking for specifics. God knew what Adam liked and who Adam was and made the woman to be able to please him in everyway. If there were another man she would not have fitted him because God made her for Adam only, which suited him in just about every way.

1. God Himself made the woman that will suit the man.
2. The woman was a part of Adam, which meant that they were compatible, having many things in common.
3. God put the woman in the garden after everything was in place so she would have nothing missing, nothing broken.
4. God made sure He brought the woman to Adam that there would be no mistaking whom she was for.
5. God was pleased that Adam was pleased.

Now, because the woman was not there when God spoke to Adam regarding the tree, the devil went to her, which brings us back to chapter 3: verses 2-3, which states:

And the woman said to the serpent, we may eat the fruit from the trees of the garden, except the fruit from the tree, which is in the middle of the garden. God has said you shall not eat of it; neither shall you touch it lest you die.

So Adam related to Eve what God had said. In verses 4-5 Satan spoke to the woman and deceived her saying:

But the serpent said to the woman, you shall not surely die. For God knows that in the day you eat of it your eyes will be opened and you will be like God, knowing the difference between good and evil and blessings and calamity.

The enemy uses different tactics to get to us. The things that we desire he brings to us to tempt us and causes us to fail.

1. He lets us think that we will gain wisdom.
2. He uses our desires for power wanting to be like God.
3. He uses our desires for an individual.
4. He uses the things that we crave.
   a. Such as wealth.
   b. Such as wisdom.
   c. Such as knowledge.
   d. Such as material things.
      1. Cars   2.Houses
      3. Lands   4.Businesses

The enemy knows what we want and he will always bring those things to us to temp us and we have to be very careful not to fall for his tricks. The enemy will do everything in his power to make you fall and to make you fail. He would go all out and even lie to you and make it look like it was the truth to make you fall for it.

THE CURSE

The enemy knows what to say to make us do what he wants us to do by telling us the things that we desire. He begins by putting greed in our hearts making us want to be like someone or something that God did not want us to be and did not design us to be. Here comes the fall of man and the loss of dominion.

Verse 6 states:

> *And when the woman saw that the tree was good (suitable, pleasant) for food and that it was delightful to look at, and a tree to be desired in order to make one wise, she took of it's fruit and ate; and she gave some also to her husband, (Adam) and he ate.*

The woman took of the fruit when she thought that the fruit was good for food and took of it and did eat. Eve had the lust of the eye,

1. When she saw it was good for food.
2. When she saw that it would make one wise.
3. When she saw that it was to make them know good and evil.
4. When she saw it was to make them like gods.

She took and gave to her husband also who did eat. What she did not know was that they were already like God and the enemy was using something against them that they were already. He used reverse psychology on her. He made her want what she already had because she did not know who she really was. She did not know that she was the image of God and she was very trusting, not knowing anything about evil and believed the trickery of the enemy. She never even thought that evil would enter into the garden to cause them to fall. She had no idea what evil was, it was the furthest thing from her mind. She was very naïve. It was not even a thought on her mind and the enemy used greed and a hunger to be like God (which she already was) to cause her to take and eat of the forbidden fruit and because of their disobedience to God, man lost everything, but there is good news. You see, God always turns a bad situation around for our good. Here's how.

Verse 15 God said: *And I will put enmity between you and the woman, and between your offspring and her Offspring; He will bruise and tread your head underfoot, and you will lie in wait and bruise His heel.*

God cursed them all three.

1. The woman was going to have child labor pains.
2. The man had to work hard toiling the ground for food.
3. The woman had to now look to the man for the things she needs.
4. The serpent was now going to crawl on its belly.
5. The serpent was going to bruise his head while the woman's seed was going to bruise His heel.
6. Satan was going to be destroyed by the second Adam (Jesus Christ).

In other words, God had another plan. He was going to send another man (which we call the second Adam) who would stand in the gap and would bruise the head of Satan and redeem us back to God. This is how Jesus came into the picture to give us back the dominion that we've lost. Since we lost dominion, man was cursed. That's why man has to work harder and women have childbirth pains, and the serpent eats dust and we hate it till this day.

God put man out of that beautiful garden and problems set in because sin entered. They had two sons, Cain (the oldest) the other named Abel. Cain slew Abel because of jealousy and the world got worse. Not what God had originally intended, but He already knew what Adam and Eve would do, so He had another plan even before the foundation of the world. God knew what He was going to do and everything that would ever happen. God was not surprised by what Adam and Eve did. He did not sit there and wonder what He was going to do next. He already had it all planned out. His plan was to send His One and only Son to save us.

CHAPTER 5
WHO JESUS REALLY IS?

In the last chapter you learned what happened to man and why we not only lost dominion but we also needed redemption. The only one who can redeem us is the Son of God whose name is JESUS. In this chapter you will learn who Jesus really is, and what He did.

In the New Testament, in the Gospel according to Luke, which is the third book of the New Testament, you will find the story of Jesus' birth. It is to let you see and know that He was born of a Virgin. Saint Johns' gospel states that He was made flesh and dwelt among us. How can God save us? It's only by Him becoming human like us that He may be able to reach us and to know the same feelings and things that we go through and face in our everyday lives.

Luke 1:26-35 states:

> *Now in the sixth month [after that], the angel Gabriel was sent from God to a town of Galilee named Nazareth, to a girl never having been married and a virgin engaged to be married to a man whose name was Joseph, a descendant of the house of David; and the virgin's name was Mary. And he came to her and said, Hail, O favored one [endued with grace]! The Lord is with you! Blessed (favored of God) are you before all other women! But when she saw him, she was greatly troubled and disturbed and confused at what he said and kept revolving in her mind what such a greeting might mean. And the angel said to her, do not be afraid, Mary, for you have found grace (free, spontaneous, absolute favor and loving-kindness) with God. And listen! You will become pregnant and will give birth to a Son, and you shall call His name Jesus. He will be great (eminent) and will be called the*

Son of the Most High; and the Lord God will give to Him the throne of His forefather David. And He will reign over the house of Jacob throughout the ages; and of His reign there will be no end. And Mary said to the angel, how can this be, since I have no [intimacy with any man as a] husband? Then the angel said to her, The Holy Spirit will come upon you, and the power of the Most High will overshadow you [like a shining cloud]; and so the Holy (pure, sinless) Thing (Offspring) which shall be born of you will be called the Son of God.

Mary went through some things believing in something that nobody else would ever believe to be true. She now faced the hardship of having to tell what had happened to her knowing how the people would treat her and what could happen to her.

1. She was a single woman who was very young.
2. She risks loosing her husband to be.
3. People would be laughing, mucking, and calling her all sorts of names.
4. She could be stoned to death for having a baby out of wedlock.

Matthew 1:21 states:

She will bear a Son, and you shall call His name Jesus [the Greek form of the Hebrew Joshua which means Savior], for He shall save His people from their sins [that is prevent them from failing and missing the true end and scope of life, which is God].

In the fourth book of the New Testament, the Gospel according to John 1-5 states:

In the beginning [before all time] was the Word (Christ), and the Word was with God, and the Word was God Himself. He was present originally with God. All things were made and came into existence through Him; and without Him was not even one thing made that has come into being. In Him was Life, and the Life was the Light of men. And the Light shines on in the darkness, for the darkness has never overpowered it [put it out or absorbed it or appropriated it and is unreceptive to it].

Jesus was there in the beginning and was pleased to come and do what He came to do.

1. He was there before the foundation of the world.
2. He made and created man.
3. He made everything that was made.
4. He is the light of the world.
5. He is the life of us all.

Verses 9-14 state:

There it was-the true Light [was then] coming into the world [the genuine, perfect, steadfast Light] that illumines every person. He came into the world, and though the world was made through Him, the world did not recognize Him [did not know Him]. He came to that which belonged to Him [to His own-His domain, creations, things, world], and they who were His own did not receive Him and did not welcome Him. But to as many as did receive and welcome Him, He gave them authority (power, privilege, right) to become the children of God, that is, to those who believe in (adhere to, trust in and rely on) His name-who owes their birth neither to blood nor to the will of the flesh [that of physical impulse] nor to the will of man [that of a natural father], but to God. [They are born of God!] And the word (Christ) became flesh (human, incarnate) and tabernacle (fixed His tent of flesh, lived awhile) among us; and we [actually] saw His glory (His honor, His majesty), such glory as in the only begotten son receives from His Father, full of grace (favor, loving-kindness) and truth.

Jesus was in a place where those who should have accepted Him were not too pleased with Him, they were jealous of Him.

1. His own rejected Him.
2. His own denied Him.
3. His own mucked and laughed at Him.
4. His own wanted to kill Him.

Although Jesus knew what would happen to Him, He was still willing to come because of how much He loved us.

Verse 17 states:

For while the law was given through Moses, (the one who God used to lead the children of Israel out of Egypt, and cross over the red sea). *Grace (unearned, undeserved favor and spiritual blessing) and truth came through Jesus Christ.*

Verses 29-34 state:

The next day John (the Baptist) saw Jesus coming to him and said, look! There is the Lamb of God, who takes away the sin of the world. This is He of whom I said, after me comes a Man who has priority over me [who takes rank above me] because He was before me and existed before I did. And I did not know Him and did not recognize Him [myself], but it is in order that He should be made manifest and be reveled to Israel [be brought out where we can see Him] that I came baptizing in with water. John gave further evidence saying I have seen the spirit descending as a dove out of heaven and it dwelt on Him [never to depart]. And I did not know Him nor recognize Him But He who sent me to baptize in (with) water said to me, upon Him whom you shall see the spirit descended and remain, that One is He who baptizes with the Holy Spirit. And I have seen [that happen-I actually did see it] and my testimony is that this is the Son of God.

Jesus is the One that was promised by God to be the One to redeem us from our sins and make us come back and have a relationship with God our Father, and He told us what to look for in His coming.

1. He was born of a virgin.
2. He was born in a stable.
3. He was born as the Son of God.
4. He was born as the savior of the world.

Now that we have established that Jesus is the Son of God born of a virgin, we have to see what His purpose for coming was, but in order to get to that we have to look at His life and what He did here on earth. Jesus taught the people, healed the sick, cast out devils and did many miracles here on earth for three and a half years. He was thirty years old when He began His ministry. In John chapter 2 Jesus did His very first miracle by turning water into wine. Jesus was on the scene three different times.

1. He showed up when He was a baby.
2. He showed up when He was twelve.
3. He showed up when He was thirty.

The first miracle Jesus did. Verses 1-11 State:

On the third day there was a wedding at Cana of Galilee, and the mother of Jesus was there. Jesus also was invited with

His disciples to the wedding. And when the wine was all gone, the mother of Jesus said to Him, they have no more wine! Jesus said to her, [dear] woman, what is that to you and to Me? [What do we have in common? Leave it to Me.] My time (hour to act) has not yet come. His mother said to the servants, whatever He says to you do it. Now there were six water pots of stone standing there, as the Jewish custom of purification (ceremonial washing) demanded, holding twenty to thirty gallons apiece. Jesus said to them, fill the water pots with water. So they filled them up to the brim. Then He said to them, draw out and take it to the manager of the feast [to the one presiding, the superintendent of the banquet]. So they took him some. And when the manager tasted the water just now turned into wine, not knowing where it came from-though the servants who had drawn the water knew-he called the bridegroom and said to him, everyone else serves the best wine first, and when people have drunk freely, then he serves that which is not so good; but you have kept back the good wine until now. This, the first of His signs (miracles, wonderworks), Jesus performed in Cana of Galilee, and manifested His glory [by it He displayed His greatness and His power openly], and His disciples believed in Him [adhered to, trusted in, and relied on Him.

The second miracle that Jesus did was to heal a nobleman's son.

In John 4:46-54 state:

So Jesus came again to Cana of Galilee, where He had turned the water into wine. And there was a certain royal official whose son was lying ill in Capernaum. Having heard that Jesus had come back from Judea into Galilee, he went away to meet Him and begin to beg Him to come down and cure his son, for he was lying at the point of death. Then Jesus said to him, unless you see signs and miracles happen, you [people] never will believe (trust, have faith) at all. The king's officer pleaded with Him, Sir, do come down at once before my little child is dead! Jesus answered him, go in peace; you son will live! And the man put his trust in what Jesus said and started home. But even as he was on the road going down, his servants met him and reported, saying, your son lives! So he asked them at what time he had begun to get better, they said, yesterday during the seventh hour (about one o'clock in the afternoon) the fever left him. Then the father knew that it was at the very hour when Jesus had said to him, your son will live. And he and his entire household believed (adhered to, trusted in, and relied on Jesus). This is the second sigh (wonderwork, miracle) that Jesus preformed after He had come out of Judea into Galilee.

In Mark 4:35-41, Jesus was on a ship and a great storm arose of strong winds and harsh waves and Jesus was in the hindermost part of the ship asleep. His disciples were very afraid and went to wake Him up saying, "carest thou not that we perish?" Jesus arose and rebuked the wind and the waves saying, "Peace be still." And there was a great calm. Jesus then asked them why were they so fearful, how was it that they had no faith because Jesus was on the ship with them. I guess they thought that they would have all drown along with Jesus. They had seen all the miracles that Jesus had done yet they were afraid and they had no faith.

Now if Jesus is telling you to go to the other side and He's in the boat with you and although a great storm may arise (which it often does), you need not be afraid because Jesus is near. He's in the boat with you. However, we do have to call for Him sometimes because we do get afraid from time to time, but as you grow in God things do not bother or worry you as much. So if He said that you are going to the other side you can rest assure that you will get there no matter how hard the enemy rages at you. The disciples feared exceedingly saying, "What manner of Man is this, that even the winds and the sea obeys Him." They yet did not come to grips or with reality that He was the Son of God. Jesus just has to speak one word to your situation and it shall be so.

Another thing that Jesus did was forgive people their wrong doings. In John 8:3-11 the religious people brought a woman to Jesus who was caught in the very act of adultery (how they knew that, only God knows). They came and told Jesus that the law says, (like He did not know the law), that they should stone to death anyone who has committed adultery (that is having sex with another other than your spouse). They asked Him what should they do seeing that she was caught in the very act, but Jesus stooping down said unto them, "you that are without sin cast the first stone" and Jesus began writing on the ground again. The religious men were pricked in their hearts because they too have sinned and they went their way starting with the oldest to the youngest. Jesus then lifted up himself and saw no man, save the woman alone, Jesus asked her, "where are thine accusers?" and she said, "Lord I have none", Jesus said unto her, "neither do I condemn you, go and sin no more."

Maybe, because you've done things in the past and people are constantly telling you about it, you begin to feel that you cannot be helped or that you will always be that way and that you cannot change. Don't let them and their words get to you, because things can and will change for the better in your life.

Here's another story of a man that Jesus encountered and his life was changed. In Luke 19:1-10, this is a story of a man name Zacchaeus, he was the chief among the publicans and he was a tax collector and was very rich. He wanted to see Jesus, but because he was little in stature he could not see, so he had an idea and ran ahead and climbed up into a tree because Jesus was going to be passing by that way. When Jesus got to where he was, Jesus looked at him and said, "Zacchaeus, come down for I must dine at your house today." Zacchaeus made haste and came down, he was surprise that Jesus wanted to spend time at his house lit-a-lone knew his name. The religious people were mad because Jesus went to eat with a sinner. At Zacchaeus house he turned to Jesus and said, "The half of my possession I will give to the poor and if I have taken anything from anyone by false accusation I will pay him back four fold." Jesus said, "Today is salvation come to this house forasmuch as he is a son of Abraham, for the son of man is come to seek and to save that which was lost."

So you see, people do change and according to bible times what Zacchaeus was, was considered the worse you can be, and he changed and so can you. Jesus came to save you, give Him your life today.

CHAPTER 6
JESUS SPOKE TO THOSE THAT OTHERS WON'T

Jesus spoke to the people that others would never speak to. He touched people that others would never touch.

Matthew 8:1-3 state:

> *When Jesus came down from the mountain great throngs followed Him. And behold, a leper came up to Him and prostrating himself, worshiped Him, saying, Lord, if you are willing, You are able to cleanse me by curing me. And He reached out His hand and touched him, saying, I am willing, be cleansed by being cured. And instantly his leprosy was cured and cleansed.*

Jesus was willing to touch the leper and heal him without ever thinking about how nasty, dirty and smelly he was.

THE ONE THAT RETURNED

Luke 17:12-19 state:

> *And as He was going into one village, He was met by ten lepers, who stood at a distance, and they raised up their voices and called, Jesus, Master take pity and have mercy on us. And when He saw them, He said unto them, go [at once] and shoe yourselves to the priests. And as they went they were cured and made clean. Then one of then upon seeing that he was cured, turned back, recognizing and thanking and praising God with a loud voice and he fell prostrate at Jesus' feet, thanking Him [over and over. And he was a Samaritan. Then Jesus asked, were not all ten cleansed? Where are the nine? Was there no one found to return and to recognize and give thanks*

and praise to God except this alien? And He said to him, get up go on your way; your faith (your trust and confidence that spring from you belief in God) has restored you to health.

You must always be grateful for what the Lord has done for you. It is vitally important that you show your appreciation to God because He wants to know that you are appreciative of Him.

1. Never be ungrateful for what Jesus has done for you.
2. Never walk away and not gave Him thanks.
3. When you see that you're healed always turn back in gratitude of praise and you will get an extra blessing.
4. When you are grateful you show Him so by just laying at His feet.

Always remember to be thankful to God for all He has done for you. Always be that one person who turns back to give God thanks. The one that returned was a Samaritan who was considered low-class in those days and the Jews had nothing to do with them. But yet he was the only one who returned and gave thanks to God.

You are going to go through, but when you're going through remember that Jesus was our example and He showed us how to overcome.

1. Jesus showed us that our storms are under our feet.
2. If we feel like we're sinking to call on Him.
3. When we call on Him, He will reach for us.
4. Not to look at the storm but to look to Him.

Jesus did more miracles in order for the people to believe that He was who they were looking for and waited on. In Matthew 14:22-33 Jesus had just fed five thousand men besides women and children. He told His disciples to go unto the other side while He sent the multitude away. As it was now wee hours in the morning, Jesus was alone on the shore and He went out to meet them.

The winds were heavy and the waters were rough and the boat was out in the middle. Jesus came walking on the water to meet them and when they saw Him they were afraid and thought it was a ghost, but Jesus said, "Do not be afraid for it is I." Peter said, "Lord if it be you bid me come on the water", Jesus said, "come." So Peter stepped out of the boat and started walking on the water to meet Jesus, but because of the heavy winds he began to be afraid and took his eyes off of Jesus and looked at the circumstances around him and he began to sink. Peter called out to Jesus saying, "Help me Lord." Now, normally if you step into your pool for instance, you will automatically sink to the bottom without having a chance to say, "help" much less "help me Lord." Jesus reached out for him immediately and they both walked back to the boat.

Life is very much the same. When we are going through our troubles and trials we stop looking to God and start looking at everything that is going on in our lives as Peter did, and things gets worse. Things take much longer only because we lose focus on God. We would have gotten out much quicker than we did had we stayed focused on God. However, just as Jesus reached out to Peter, so Jesus will reach out to you when you call on His name. He did not let Peter drown and He will not let you, either.

JESUS FED THE MULTITUDE

Jesus also fed the multitude of people not only once but twice. This was to let us know that if we are hungry He will also feed us from the little that we have. There's nothing that God cannot do.

Mark 6:35-44 states:

And when the day was already far-gone, His disciples came to Him and said, this is a desolate and isolated place, and the hour is now late. Send the crowds away to go into the country and villages round about and buy themselves something to eat. But He [Jesus] replied to them, give them something to eat yourselves. And they said to Him, shall we go and buy 200 denarii's [about 40 dollars] worth of bread and give it to them to eat? and He said to them, how many loaves do you have? Go and see. And when they [had looked and] knew, they said, five [loaves] and two fish. Then He commanded that the people all to recline on the grass by companies. So they threw themselves down in rank of hundreds and fifties [with the regularity of an arrangement of beds of herds looking like so many garden plots]. And taking the five loaves and two fish, He looked up to heaven and, praising God, gave thanks and broke the loves and kept on giving them to the disciples to set before the people; and He [also] divided the two fish among [them] all. And they all ate and were satisfied. And they took up twelve [small hand] baskets full of broken pieces [from the loves] and of the fish. And they that eat the loves were 5000 men.

Jesus told the disciples to make the people do something since He was going to feed them. They had to follow directions. Then He (Jesus) had to do some things before He could feed them.

1. He made them to sit down.
2. He took the bread and the fishes and blessed them.
3. He then broke and gave to His disciples.
4. His disciples gave to the people.
5. They picked up 12 baskets full of leftovers.

In Mark 8:1-9 Jesus also fed 4000 people with only seven loves and a few small fish. The people were with Jesus for three days and they had nothing to eat; they just sat and heard His words. Jesus again wanted to feed them and his disciples had forgotten about the feeding of the 5000. When Jesus said to feed them, they again said that it was going to cost too much money. They then brought what they had and Jesus again blessed it, broke it, and gave it to the disciples and they all ate; and they picked up seven baskets that remained. The difference with this feeding was that they were hungry to hear the words of Jesus so they stayed for days in His presence just to hear Him. Although they had nothing to eat, they were willing to go hungry just to hear Him. Are you hungry to hear Him? How hungry are you? Are you hungry for His presence and are you willing to stay in His presence?

This is how Jesus will work in your life. He will take what you've got and He will multiply it and cause you to have much more than you dreamed possible. When you are hungry for Him, He will feed you and you will be satisfied.

THE LOST

In Luke 15:4-24 Jesus tells us three parables: One of a lost coin, one of a lost sheep, and one of a lost boy. The difference between the three is that if a coin gets lost you have to look for it, and if a sheep gets lost you have to do the same thing—you have to look for it. But the difference between those things and a boy is that the boy can remember where he was and can find his way back.

Luke 15:11-24 states:

> *There was a certain man who had two sons; and the younger of them said to his father, Father, give me the part of the property that falls [to me]. And he divided the estate between*

them. And not many days after that, the younger son gathered up all he had and journeyed into a distant country, and there he wasted his fortune in reckless and loose living. And when he had spent all he had, a mighty famine came upon that country, and he began to fall behind and be in want. So he went and forced himself upon one of the citizens of that country, who sent him to his fields to feed hogs (pigs, swine). And he would have gladly have fed on and fill hid belly with the carob pods that the hogs were eating, but they could not satisfy his hunger and nobody gave him anything. Then when he came to himself, he said, how many hired servants of my father have enough food, and to spear, but I am perishing (dying) of hunger. I will get up and go to my father, and I will say to him, father, I have sinned against heaven and in your sight. I am no longer worthy to be called your son, make me like one of your hired servants. So he got up and came to his father. But while he was still a long way off, his father saw him and was moved with pity and tenderness; and he ran and embraced him and kissed him. And the son said to him, father I have sinned against heaven and in your sight; I am no longer worthy to be called your son, but the father said to his bond servants, bring quickly the best robe and put it on him, and give him a ring for his hand and sandals for his feet. And bring out a fatted calf and kill it and let us revel and feast and be happy and make merry, because this my son was dead and is alive again; he was lost and is found! And they began to revel and feast and make merry.

When you come to God you get all the benefits of being one of His own.

1. You become a King's kid.
2. You get to dress in royalty.
3. You get a mark that the enemy knows that you're God's.
4. You get a feast in your honor.

5. You get to be partaker of His inheritance.
6. You get to be like Him.
    a. Look like Him.
    b. Love like Him.
    c. Walk like Him.
    d. Talk like Him.
    e. Wisdom like Him.
    f. Overcome like Him.
    g. Authority like Him.
7. You get to live with Him for all eternity.

This is a reflection of our heavenly Father. He will do the same for you. What the young man did not know was that the day he left home his father went outside saying, "this is the day my son will come home." He repeats that saying day after day. That's why he was able to see his son a far way off because every day he was looking for him to come home. His father did not give up hope that his son will one day return. His father did not even wait for him to get close but ran to him with outstretched arms and kissed him. Although he was dirty and smelly, it did not bother the father one bit to throw his arms around him and kiss him. Then you see how he arrayed him in fine clothes and put a ring and robe on him signifying royalty. He wanted to be a servant, but he was still his father's son. Then they killed the best and had a party.

That's how our heavenly Father is; when those that are lost come back to Him and give Him or rededicate their lives to Him, He celebrates our return. He looks for you every day waiting with open arms. It does not matter where you've been; it does not matter what you've done, all that matters is that you come back to Him. He will dress you with royalty and give you more than you ever dreamed possible. The angels will rejoice when you come back to God. They will throw a party in your honor.

Don't be afraid. Just as this young man recognized his mistake and went back home, you also need not only to recognize your mistakes, but also get up, and turn your life back to the only One who truly cares for you. He's waiting with open arms to welcome you back. Tell yourself, "There's more to me than meets the eye. I have someone who cares. I am royalty. I am a child of God and He loves me." He will make what's wrong in your life right all in due time. All you have to do is come

CHAPTER 7
JESUS RAISED THE DEAD

Jesus also raised the dead showing forth His power as Him being the resurrection and the Life.

John 11:25 state, *I am the Resurrection and the Life. Whosoever believes in Me, although he may die, yet shall he live.*

In verses 38-45 Jesus raised Lazarus from the dead after he was dead for four days; and the people who saw believed in Him.

> *Now Jesus, again sighing repeatedly and deeply disquieted, approached the tomb. It was a cave (a hole in the rock), and a boulder lay against [the entrance to close] it. Jesus said, take away the stone. Martha the sister of the dead man, exclaimed, But Lord, by this time he [is decaying and] throws off an offensive odor, for he has been dead four days! Jesus said to her, Did I not tell you and promise you that if you would believe and rely on Me, you would see the glory of God? So they took away the stone. And Jesus lifted up His eyes and said, Father, I thank You that You have heard Me. Yes, I know You always hear and listen to Me, but I have said this on account of and for the benefit of the people standing around, so that they may believe that You did send Me [that You have made Me Your messenger]. When He said this, He shouted with a loud voice, Lazarus, come out! And out walked the man who had been dead, his hands and feet wrapped in burial cloths (linen strips), and with a [burial] napkin bound around his face. Jesus said to them, Free him of the burial wrappings and let him go. Upon seeing what Jesus had done, many of the Jews who had come with Mary believed in Him. [They trusted in Him and adhere to Him and relied on Him.]*

Whatever your situation, although you may think that you cannot make a comeback or even live again after that situation, whatever it may be, when you come to Jesus He will raise you again from the dead. He will give you life and more abundantly.

In John 14:1-2 Jesus states, *Do not let your hearts be troubled (distressed, agitated). You believe in and adhere to and trust in and rely on God; believe in and adhere to and trust in and rely on Me.*

In verse 6 Jesus state, *I am the Way and the Truth and the Life; no one comes to the Father except by (through) Me.*

Jesus said, "If you love Me you will keep my commandments." What are these commandments? As children no one taught us how to lie or steal, but when we did we knew it was wrong or else we would not be trying to hide what we stole behind our backs. How did we know it was wrong when no one told us it was wrong? The reason being, before we were born it was written in our hearts, because we were born in sin and shapen in iniquity, according to Psalm 51:5. God in His infinite wisdom and mercies placed right and wrong in our hearts. Moses ran from Pharaoh into the backside of the desert before God gave him the Ten Commandments. These things existed in our hearts. It was already there; that if and when we would sin, we would be convicted. That is why we try to do something about it, whether it is running and hiding, as Moses did, or a child hiding the things behind his or her back.

THE TEN COMMANDMENTS

In Exodus 20:3-7 God gave Moses the 10 commandments when they were up in Mount Sinai saying:

1. *Thou shall have no other gods before Me.*

2. *Thou shalt not make any graven image.*
3. *Thou shalt not take the Lord thy God name in vain.*
4. *Remember the saboth day and keep it holy.*
5. *Honor thy father and thy mother.*
6. *Thou shalt not kill.*
7. *Thou shalt not commit adultery.*
8. *Thou shalt not steal.*
9. *Thou shalt not bear false witness.*
10. *Thou shalt not covet thy neighbor's wife.*

In Matthew 22:37-40 Jesus states:

> *Thou shalt love the Lord your God with all your heart, and with all your soul, and with all your mind (intellect). This is the great (most important, principle) and first commandment. And the second is like it: you shall love your neighbor as [you do] yourself. These two commandments sum up, and upon them depend, all the law and the prophets.*

If you keep these commandments,

1. You will please God and get His love and protection.
2. You will live a long and prosperous life.
3. Your children will be blessed.
4. You will have abundant life.

Why did Jesus use only these two commandments? It's because if you love God more than anything and or even anyone, then you will automatically love yourself. In turn, you will treat your neighbors the right way, because the love of God is actually flowing through you to them. If you love God with all your heart, you will be good to those that He loves. God is the actual One that will help you to do those things you think are too hard for you to do. He makes it easier to love those who are hard to love. He makes you treat your enemies the right way even if you don't want to. God is forever loving, good and kind. He will always show you love and He will always be disappointed if you do not show it back to others. When you truly love, you will not hurt your neighbor in anyway.

1. You will not lie about your neighbor.
2. You will not steal from them or want what they have with envy and jealousy.
3. You will not commit adultery, or even curse out your neighbor.
4. You will automatically want what's best for your neighbor.
5. You will pray for them and just be nice, period.

Once you love God the way you aught, you would not even think of harming anyone, you would love them also. God will be so full in you that there will be no room for hate.

YOUR NEIGHBORS

So who is your neighbor? I'm not just talking about the person who lives next door to you; that's not what the bible is speaking about.

Luke 10:29-37 states:

> *And he determined to acquit himself pf reproach, said to Jesus, and who is my neighbor? Jesus taking him up replied, a certain man was going from Jerusalem down to Jericho, and he fell among robbers, who stripped him of his cloths and belongings and beat him and went their way, [unconcernedly] leaving him half dead, as it happened. Now by coincidence a certain priest was going down along that road, and when he saw him, he passed on the other side. A Levite likewise came*

down to the place and saw him, and passed by on the other side [of the road]. But a certain Samaritan, as he traveled along, came down to where he was; and when he saw him, he moved with pity and sympathy [for him]. And went to him and dressed his wounds, pouring on [them] oil and wine. Then he set him on his own beast and brought him to an inn and took care of him. And the next day he took out two denarii's [two days wages] and gave [them] to the innkeeper, saying, take care of him; and whatever more you spend, I [myself] will repay you when I return. Which of these three do you think proved himself a neighbor to him who fell among the robbers? He answered, the one who showed pity and mercy to him. And Jesus said to him, go and do likewise

Those who do good to others are considered more neighborly. It's speaking about the people you come in contact with on a day-to-day basis.

1. They are the people you see in the supermarket.
2. They are the people you work with at your job.
3. They are the people you see at the movies.
4. They are the people you see on the streets.
5. They are the people at your church.

Anywhere you go and whomever you see, they are your neighbors. Just people in general. But how can we love God in that way when we cannot see Him? Jesus said, "How can you say you love God who you cannot see and hate your brother who you can see." Jesus went on to say that the truth is not in you if you say you love God and hate your brother.

Jesus said in John 14:21:

The person who has My commands and keeps them is the one who [really] loves Me; and whoever [really] loves Me will be loved by my Father, and I [too] will love him and will show (reveal, manifest) Myself to him.

If we really love God we will keep His commandments and He will bless us in return for being faithful to Him and for loving Him. He will also show up and show out in our lives.

Verse 24 states: *Anyone who does not [really] love Me does not observe and obey My teaching. And the teaching, which you hear and heed, is not Mine, but [comes] from the Father who sent me.*

If we do not love Him, we are none of His and He will not love us if we keep on refusing Him. We would be lost and stay lost if we do not turn our lives around. Jesus throughout the entire gospel told us not only how to love, but also how to please Him. He told us who He is, and what He came to do. That was to seek and to save that which is lost. We were all lost at one time or another before Jesus reached down and found us and took us out of the gutter. The key to after being saved is abiding in Him.

ABIDING IN HIM

What does it mean to abide in Him and how do we abide in Him?

In John 15:5 states: *I am the vine; you are the branches, whoever lives in Me and I in him bears much (abundant) fruit. However, apart from Me [cut of from vital union with Me] you can do nothing.*

If we do not remain in Him, we will fall right back into sin and we will not grow in God. How do we abide in Him?

1. We abide in Him by praying every day.

2. We abide in Him by spending ample amount of time reading His word.
3. We abide in Him by singing, praising, and worshiping Him when things are good and even if they are bad.
4. We abide in Him by meditating on Him day and night.

The book of Psalm is a good place to start reading to get your praise and worship on. You will hear these two things (prayer and reading the word) throughout this book. It is vital for your growth and development in God. You will not know Him until you spend time with Him. He wants you more than you want Him and He will give you the time if you ask it of Him. All you have to do is ask.

Luke 11:9-10 states:

> *So I say to you ask, and keep on asking and it shall be given you; seek and keep on seeking and you shall find; knock and keep on knocking and the door shall be opened to you. For everyone who ask and keeps on asking receives; and he who seeks and keep on seeking finds; and to him who knocks and keep on knocking, the door shall be opened.*

When you pray do not give up? because He said, "If you ask, seek and knock that you would get an answer." It may not be when you expect it to be, but remember that God knows best and He is always right on time.

1. Ask—God said to ask and when you do He will answer. If you do not ask you will not get. You also have to ask until it comes to pass. God will hear and answer if it is according to His will for your life.

   a. Ask God directly for what you want.
   b. Ask God without being shy.

      c. Ask God not just for yourself.

      d. Ask God to show you His will.

2. Seek—God said if you seek you will find. You need to seek God and He will be found. God wants to be with you but He gives you a chance to see how much you want what you're seeking. He does not come easily. You have to seek with all your heart and seek Him early. Persevere, then you will find Him.

      a. Seek God earnestly.

      b. Seek God every day.

      c. Seek God for others.

      d. Seek God lovingly.

3. Knock—God said if you knock it shall be opened to you. Know what door you are knocking on. You do not want to knock on a door that is not yours that might be too much or too little for you to handle. God only opens doors that are assigned, destined, and designed just for you. So if the door is not opening it could mean it is somebody else's door you're knocking on.

      a. Knock desperately.

      b. Knock vigorously.

      c. Knock until it opens and if it does not open.

          i.   It may be the wrong door.

          ii.   You may not be ready.

          iii. It may not be the right time.

          iv. It could be that you missed your own opened door, but it will come around again in due time.

So whatever it is that you need, all you have to do is ask God, and He will grant it according to His will. Do not just ask in order to use it upon your own lust, but ask Him where it glorifies Him. He will answer; keep on asking, seeking, and knocking.

James 4:2-3 states:

> *You are jealous and covet [what others have] and your desires are unfulfilled; [so] you become murderers. [To hate is to murder as far as your hearts are concerned.] You burn with envy and anger and are not able to obtain [the gratification, the contentment, and the happiness that you seek, so you fight and war. You do not have, because you do not ask. Or you do ask [God for them] and yet fail to receive, because you ask with wrong purpose and evil, selfish motives. Your intension is [when you get what you desire] to spend it in sensual pleasures.*

So when you ask, make sure you are asking for the right reasons. You will not receive if you do not. God wants to give you things. He wants us to be happy and to live an abundant life with more than enough, but we must first come to Him the right way and with a right attitude.

CHAPTER 8
GOD WANTS US TO BE LIKE JESUS

God wants us to be saved and to be like His Son, Jesus. Jesus came for a reason and a purpose. It is not His will for us to perish but that all should come to repentance according to 2Peter 3:9. God wants us back. He wants to have a relationship with you and you with Him. That is why He sent His One and only Son for you and for me. These are just four reasons Jesus was born.

1. He was born to redeem mankind.
2. He was born to die.
3. He was born to save us from ourselves and from our sinful ways.
4. He was born to reconcile us back to God.

He wants you no matter what state you're in. Whatever the condition, He still wants you. His love for you is everlasting. However bad you may be, have been, God still loves you and wants you.

You cannot clean up yourself on your own. You cannot say, "Well, let me get this particular area in my life right first, then I will come to God." In that case you will never come to God. Thank God it does not work that way. You cannot clean up yourself by yourself. God has to help you clean up yourself. Give it to God and watch Him work in your life. If you don't repent and give it to Him, you will perish.

In Luke 13:2-5 Jesus states:

> *Do you think that these Galileans were greater sinners than all the other Galileans because they have suffered in this way? I tell you, no; but unless you repent (change your mind for the better and heartily amend your ways, with abhorrence of your*

past sins), you will all likewise perish and be lost eternally. Or those eighteen on whom the tower of Siloam fell and killed them-do you think that they were more guilty offenders (debtors) than all the others who dwelt in Jerusalem? I tell you, no; but on less you repent (change your mind for the better and heartily amend you ways, with abhorrence of your past sins), you will all likewise perish and be lost eternally.

Jesus wants you to repent of whatever sin it is that's in your life. He made it clear that if you do not repent, you shall perish. He's given us many chances to repent. Why not take this opportunity to do so?

In Matthew 7:13-14 Jesus spoke on the straight and wide gates. He said, *Enter through the narrow gate; for wide is the gate and specious and broad is the way that leads away to destruction, and many are those you are entering through it.*

You see, it's easier to sin than to do the right thing. Many people want to do whatever the world is doing (including Christians), because they want to be in the clique. The broad way and the wide gate is the road (path) leading to destruction (hell). There are no obstacles or hindrances on the way. You can do whatever you want without restriction. Be careful what you do, it might just get you a ticket to hell. Trust me; you do not want to go there. It is for eternity that you will be there; that's a long time. On earth you live a hundred or so years but eternity is forever. Jesus also went on to say, *But the gate is narrow (contracted by pressure) and the way is straitened and compressed that leads away to life, and few are those who find it.*

This means that the things that are right, and those who do not wish to do wrong, but follow the things of God and adhere to them and not want to be in the clique and to be accepted by others, they are few and far between. That's not good enough. We need more voices to let the world know the truth. People are dying and going to hell because holiness is no longer being preached in the churches, but I am here to tell you, it is holiness or hell. Not enough people are finding the narrow road (path). They are not being taught properly how to find it and how to stay on it. The broad way is so broad, and it seems to get broader where too many people are finding it easier and easier because they want the easy way out. This will last only so long; we do not have eternity to fix it. We have only this life; however, long it may be, and there is no guarantee that you will even live to see tomorrow. We need to stand up and let people know it's wrong what they are doing. We need to help them find the narrow way because it leads to life and they need to know how to get there.

In Mark 13 Jesus spoke regarding signs of when He will come again. Oh, He will come again. The question is, will you be ready? You will die one day. Death is inevitable.

In Hebrews 9:27 states: *And just as it is appointed for [all] men once to die, and after that the [certain] judgment.*

The question again to you is, will you be ready? Your life should be important enough to you to want to know where you will spend eternity. Here are some questions that you need to answer.

1. How important is your life?
2. What is most important to you?
3. Is your life worth living?
4. How badly do you want what it is that you're pursuing?
5. What are you willing to do to make your life work?
6. Is what you're pursuing what God wants you to do?

These are important question for you to answer. What would you say to God when He asks you what you did and have done with My Son Jesus? Would you say,

1. I was too busy trying to make money.
2. I did not really believe the stories about Jesus.
3. I never heard the gospel before.
4. I was trying to make my life work.
5. I did not understand what they were talking about.
6. I was abused as a child, and that causes me to shut down.

Well, what would you say to Him? No matter what you say, God will take no excuses. He knows you inside and out. He knows you better than you know yourself.

Psalm 139:1-5 states:

O Lord, You have searched me [thoroughly] and have known me. You know my down sitting and my uprising; You understandest my thought afar off. You sift and search out my path and my lying down, and You are acquainted with all my ways. For there is not a word in my tongue [still unuttered], but, behold, O Lord, You know it altogether. You have beset me and shut me in-behind and before, and you have laid Your hand upon me.

All your thoughts, your innermost secrets God already knows and He still wants to make your life work for you. What if I told you that if you were to get on a plane to go somewhere to another state or country, but before you get to your destination the plane you were on was going to crash. Some will survive, but there was no guarantee that you would be the one to survive, would you still get on that plane? Now, if I tell you that you will die some day (which I already know that you know this) and that there is a ten percent chance that hell is real, are you willing to take that chance and die without knowing Jesus as Lord and Savior of your life when you know there is something you could do about it now? What do you have to loose? Only your soul. Those of us who have not accepted Jesus as Lord and Savior of our lives are hell-bound. That is not to be taken lightly. It's a serious matter. Jesus came to rescue us from that place and we need to take advantage of it.

WHAT IS HELL?

You're probably asking, what is hell? Everyone has an idea what hell is or at least his or her own perception of what it is. For instance, you might be going through something and you use the phrase, "I'm going through hell." Or the sun is very hot today and you may say, "It's hot as hell today." So we all have some idea of hell and it's always a bad thing and not a good one that we associate it with. Hell is always something bad that happens, happened or will happen to us that was or would always be negative. Hell is a place of torment, a place of eternal punishment and great suffering.

Luke 16: 19-25 states:

> *There was a certain rich man who [habitually] clothed himself in purple and fine linen and reveled and feasted and made merry in splendor every day. And at his gate there was [carelessly] dropped down and left a certain destitute man named Lazarus, [reduce to begging alms and] covered with [ulcerated] sores. He [eagerly] desired to be satisfied with what fell from the rich man's table; moreover, the dogs even came and licked his sores. And it occurred that the man [reduced to] begging died and was carried by the angels to Abraham's bosom. The rich man also died and was buried. And in Hades (the realm of the dead), being in torment, he lifted up his eyes and saw Abraham far away and Lazarus in his bosom. And he cried out and said, Father Abraham, have pity and mercy on me and send Lazarus to dip the tip of his finger in water and cool my tongue, for I am in anguish in this flame.*

But Abraham said, child, remember that you in your lifetime fully received [what is due you in] comforts and delights, and Lazarus in like manner the discomforts and distresses; but now he is comforted here and you are in anguish.

Hell is a place of punishment for the wicked. Hell was created for the devil (Satan) and his angels. These are the angels that God cast out of heaven along with the archangel, Lucifer who is now known as the devil and Satan.

In 2 Peter 2:4 states: *For God did not [even] spare angels that sinned, but cast them into hell, delivering them to be kept there in pits of gloom till the judgment and their doom.*

In the book of Revelations, which is the last book of the bible it talks about, not only what would happen to the devil and the fallen angels, but it also speaks of hell and where we would end up if we do not follow God.

Revelation 20:10 states:

Then the devil who had led them astray [deceiving and seducing them] was hurled into the fiery lake of burning brimstone, where the beast and false prophet were; and they will be tormented day and night forever and ever (through the ages of the ages).

The enemy that troubled us shall be cast into hell, but those that did not obey God in Revelation 20:13 states:

And the sea delivered up the dead who were in it, death and Hades [hell] (the state of death or disembodied existence) surrendered the dead in them, and all were tried and their cases determined by what they had done (according to their motives, aims, and works).

So hell will give up the dead and the seas also to be judged by God for their works whether they were good or bad. Everyone will stand before God and give an account of the way they lived their lives while on earth, and what you've done will determine where you spend eternity.

Revelation 20:14-15 states:

> *Then death and Hades (the state of death or disembodied existence) were thrown in the lake of fire. This is the second death, the lake of fire. And if anyone's [name] was not found recorded in the Book of Life, he was hurled into the lake of fire.*

Hell was designed only for the devil and his imps, but because we have turned our backs on God and do not want to serve Him it became a place where we would spend eternity.

1. Hell was made for the devil and his angels that fell from grace, which we call demons.
2. Hell was made as a place of punishment.
3. Hell was made for those people who are an enemy of God.
4. Hell was made for those people who reject Jesus as Lord and Savior.
5. Hell was made for those who do not follow God's commandments and want to live anyhow and think they are still in the will of God.

When you die and your name is not found in the Book, which is the Lambs Book of life, those people will spend eternity in hell tormented by the devil and his angels.

Revelation 21:8 states:

But as for the cowards and the ignoble and the contemptible and the cravenly lacking in courage and the cowardly submissive, and as for the unbelieving and faithless, and as for the depraved and defiled with abominations, and as for murderers and the lewd and adulterous and the practicers of magic arts and the idolaters (those who give supreme devotion to anyone or anything other than God) and all liars (those who knowingly convey untruth by word or deed)-[all of these shall have] their part in the lake that blaze with fire and brimstone. This is the second death.

Whatever you do that is not pleasing to God, when the end of time comes and you have not repented of all your wrongful deeds, this is the place where you will live for all eternity. It's a place where you definitely do not want to be. You think this place where you live is hell? Think again. The real one is a billion times worse.

Jesus spoke numerous times in Mark 9:43-48 where the worms dieth not and the fire is never quenched. It does not sound like a place I want to go. Do you? He spoke that if any part of you offends you, cut it off because it is better that you have one hand, one foot, one eye and enter into heaven than to have all your body parts and be thrown or cast into hell. In other words, do whatever you can to rectify your situation in your life before you lose your life to a place that was meant for only the devil and his angels, a place where even they do not want to go.

JESUS THE MISSING PIECE

You may be having a lot of fun now and your life is great, and you may have a lot of money, yet you feel something is missing. You try to fix or fill that missing feelings with more things such as cars, homes, a person, a job, or you may be always saying, "If I get this then I will be happy, or if I get that then I will be happy." Then when you do get those things you're still unhappy. There's still that something missing. You're still miserable and you're wondering why. That's because you're trying to fill a spot that only Jesus can fill. That spot is the size and shape of Jesus. Trying to fill it, or fit a different shape other than Him into it will not work. You will still be miserable. Jesus, you ask, who is Jesus? Well, Jesus is the Son of God who came into this world to seek and to save us from our sins. He is God who became man (flesh) to redeem us back to Himself. Jesus is that shape you are looking for to fill your life. Now that you know who and what it is that you're really missing, all you have to do is to try Him.

Once you try Him, you will see that it fits the exact spot that you've been looking for all your life. You will even beat yourself up as I did for not knowing or doing this sooner. You will say, "Why did I not try Jesus before? My life would have been so much better that much sooner?" Jesus loves you and He wants you to be happy and at peace. Life becomes much more meaningful when you allow Him to come in. You see, He's a gentleman; He will not force Himself upon you. He will give you the chance and opportunity to choose Him on your own. When you do, you will not only look better, but you will also feel better. People who you knew would not even recognize you.

1. Your attitude changes.
2. Your way of thinking changes.
3. Your habits change.
4. The places you go change.
5. The people you hang out with change.

The people around you will notice it too. They will notice the difference and you will end up liking yourself more. Jesus said that He has come to give us life more abundantly, according to John 10:10. We all want abundant life. We all want to be happy. We all want peace and tranquility, but we can find it only in Jesus Christ.

CHAPTER 9
SIGNS OF THE TIME

In chapter 8, I mentioned Mark chapter 13 regarding signs of when Jesus said that He was coming again. These are the things He said that you should expect.

Verses 5-8 states: *And Jesus began to tell them, be careful and watchful that no one misleads you. Many will come in [appropriating to themselves] the name [of messiah], saying, I am [He]! And they will mislead many.*

You will not be deceived because you know now what the bible says. Jesus came only once, a little over 2000 years ago. He will not come again as a man but only in the clouds, and those people who are Christians (believers in Him and who keep His words and those who truly love Him) shall be caught up to meet Him in the air. He went on to say,

> *And when you hear of wars and rumors of wars, do not get alarmed (trouble and frightened); it is necessary [that these things] take place, but the end is not yet. For nation will rise against nation, and kingdom against kingdom. There will be earthquakes in various places; there will be famines and calamities. This is the beginning of the intolerable anguish and suffering [only the first of the birth pangs].*

In the last days there will be many wars going on and there is nothing that anyone can or will be able to do about them. We do not like now what is happening with all the wars, all the fires, all the earthquakes, and all the hurricanes; but Jesus said that it has to be so. That's not all. That's just the tip of the iceberg.

Verse 10 states: *And the good news (the gospel) must first be preached to all nations.*

Well, you are reading it right now in this book so you cannot tell God that you have not heard the gospel. His words must reach everyone all over. Wherever people are, they must hear what Jesus has done for them to give them a better and an eternal life.

Verses 12-13 states:

> *And brother will hand over brother to death, and the father his child; and children will take a stand against their parents and [have] them put to death. And you will be hated and detested by everybody for My namesake, but he who patiently perseveres and endures to the end will be saved (made a partaker of the salvation by Christ, and delivered from spiritual death).*

This simply means that people would blame each other in order to save themselves from certain death, but if you are still living when this happens (and there is no guarantee that you will be), Jesus said that if you do not succumb (that is, to give in to) pressure or temptation to their will and do what they want and endure whatever hardship it is and or even die for the cause of Christ, you shall be saved.

Verses 19-22 states:

> *For at that time there will be such affliction (oppression and tribulation) as has not been from the beginning of the creation, which God created until this particular time-and positively never, will be [again]. And unless God had shortened the days, no human being will be saved (rescued); but for the sake of the elect, His chosen ones (those who He picked out for Himself), He (God) has shortened the days. And then if any one says to you, see, here is the Christ (the Messiah)! Or, look, there He is! Do not believe it. False Christ (Messiahs) and false prophets will arise and show signs and [work] miracles*

to deceive and lead astray, if possible, even the elect (those God had chosen out for Himself).

Things would be so bad that God Himself would have to shorten the day because no one would be able to stand the hardship. It would be so hard that people would not be able to bear it. People who do not know and understand Jesus would be fooled into thinking that He has come again showing forth signs and wonders, but He has forewarned you letting you know that He will not come again as a mere man. The devil is a copycat; he will copy the things Jesus did when He was on earth. There will be a hunger for signs and wonders, and people will think that the one that is doing these things is God and will welcome him and worship him. The Christians also shall be martyred (beheaded) for the kingdom of God sake.

In verses 24-27 states:

> *But in those days, after [the affliction and oppression and distress of] that tribulation, the sun will be darkened, and the moon will not give its light. And the stars will be falling from the sky, and the powers in the heavens will be shaken. And then they will see the Son of Man coming in clouds with great (kingly) power and glory (majesty and splendor). And then He will send out the angels and will gather together His elect (those He had picked out for Himself) from the four winds, from the farthest bounds of the earth to the farthest bounds of heaven.*

So God will gather the people that are His, those that accepted His Son Jesus, leaving those who did not accept Him. If you notice, these things are already happening. The signs are everywhere, and yet it's nothing compared to what will happen in those days. Jesus Himself said that there was not a time as horrific or horrendous as this. Don't be alarmed, He will and is giving you an opportunity to accept and serve Him.

Verse 33 states, *Be on you guard [constantly alert], and watch and pray for you do not know when the time will come.*

He will come suddenly as a thief in the night. Your heart needs to be right with God at all times. Do not be like the five foolish virgins who were left behind because they were not ready when the bridegroom came. You do not know when you are going to die. You do not know when Jesus would burst through the clouds. You are not sure that you would be alive when this happens. You do not want to be unprepared. You always have to be ready.

Matthew 25:1-13 states:

> *Then the kingdom of heaven shall be likened to ten virgins who took their lamps and went to meet the bridegroom. Five of them were foolish (thoughtless, without forethought) and five were wise (sensible, intelligent, and prudent). For when the foolish took their lamps they did not take any [extra] oil with them. But the wise took flasks of extra oil with them [also] with their lamps. While the bridegroom lingered and was slow in coming, they all began nodding their heads, and they fell asleep. But at midnight there was a shout, behold the bridegroom! Go out to meet him! then all those virgins got up and put their own lamps in order. And the foolish said to the wise, give us some of your oil, for our lamps are going out. But the wise replied, there will not be enough for us and for you; go instead to the dealers and buy for yourselves. But while they were gone away to buy, the bridegroom came, and those who were prepared went in with him to the marriage feast; and the door was shut. Later the other virgins also came and said, Lord, Lord, open [the door] to us! But he replied, I solemnly declare to you, I do not know you [I am not acquainted with*

you]. Watch therefore [give strict attention and be cautious and active], for you know neither the day nor the hour when the Son of Man will come.

Do not allow yourself to be left behind

1. Always keep your lamp burning.
2. Always be on the lookout for Christ's coming.
3. Always be prepared for the unexpected.
4. Always sleep with extra oil beside you (the Holy Spirit).

Although they all fell asleep, the five wise virgins brought extra oil to always keep their lamps burning (which represents the Holy Spirit). The five foolish virgins did not anticipate that He might have taken longer to come and was not prepared let their lamps burn out. When the bridegroom finally arrived, the five foolish virgins were in the shop busy buying oil.

Luke 12:35-40 states:

Keep your loins girded and your lamps burning. And be like men who are waiting for their master to return home from the marriage feast, so that when he returns from the wedding and comes and knocks, they may open to him immediately. Blessed (happy, fortunate, and to be envied) are those servants whom the master finds awake and alert and watching when he comes. Truly I say to you, he will gird himself and have them recline at table and will come and serve them! If he comes in the second watch (before midnight) or the third watch (after midnight), and finds them so, blessed (happy, fortunate, and to be envied) are those servants! But of this be assured: if the householder had known at what time the burglar was coming, he would have been awake and alert and watching and would not have permitted his house to be dug through and broken into. You also must be ready, for the

*Son of Man is coming at an hour and a moment when you
do not anticipate it.*

So you always have to be prayed up. Now that you know what
to look for, what is your heart telling you? Yes, there is a lot to
know, but as you read the bible and pray every day, God will help
you to understand it, and it will no longer be a mystery to you.
Only God can give you the interpretation of the bible anyway
because they are His words. By reading and praying, you will get
better equipped, you will be stronger in your faith. You will be
able to speak the words to someone else. You will know what the
truth is if someone else comes to you with any other doctrine.
You will grow and be more Christ-like: Spiritually, Mentally,
Emotionally, Physically, and Psychologically. You will be able to
speak the word to your circumstances and watch them go away.
You will be able to speak to the enemy and cause him to flee. For
those who are already Christians or claim to be saved, how does
your life stack up? Do not be ashamed, God already knows how
you stack up. No Christian wants to go to hell. We know and
believe that hell is real just like heaven is real. I urge you to get
your life right with God. Take a good inventory of your life. Do
not overlook anything. Be honest with yourself. It's your life. Get
it right (corrected) right now. Tomorrow may be too late.

Luke 11:29-32 states:

> *Now as the crowds were [increasingly] thronging Him, He
> began to say, This present generation is a wicked one; it seeks
> and demands a sign (miracle), but no sign shall be given to it
> except the sign of Jonah [the profit]. For [just] as Jonah became
> a sign to the people of Nineveh, so will also the Son of Man
> be [a sign] to this age and generation. The queen of the South
> will arise in the judgment with the people of this age and
> generation and condemn them; for she came from the ends of
> the [inhabited] earth to listen to the wisdom of Solomon, and*

notice, here is more than Solomon. The men of Nineveh will appear as witness at the judgment with this generation and will condemn it; for they repented at the preaching of Jonah, and behold, here is more than Jonah.

We're all looking for some kind of supernatural miracle and not looking at what is already in existence. The signs are everywhere.

1. There shall be diverse earthquakes all over the nation including the seas.
2. There shall be wars and rumors of wars.
3. Nations shall rise up against nations.
4. Kingdoms shall rise up against Kingdoms.
5. There shall be many famines in the land.
6. There shall be pestilence.
7. We shall be most hated of all nations for the name of Christ.
8. People shall betray one another and shall hate one another.
9. Many false prophets shall rise, and shall deceive many.
10. The love of many shall wax cold.
11. Many shall fall away from the faith.

Do not ignore these signs and make sure you are ready also because you do not know when the end will be. God showed me one time where many people were lined up to exit His presence and His protection and to succumb to the will of the enemy, and they did not even know it or even recognize that they are about to backslide.

Matthew 24:15 states:

So when you see the appalling sacrilege [the abomination that astonishes and makes desolate], spoken of by the prophet

Daniel, standing in the Holy Place-let the reader take notice and ponder and consider and heed [this].

Verse 29-31 states:

Immediately after the tribulation of those days the sun will be darkened, and the mood will not shed it's light, and the stars will fall from the sky, and the powers of the heavens will be shaken. Then the sign of the Son of Man will appear in the sky, and then all the tribes of the earth will mourn and beat their breasts and lament in anguish, and they will see the Son of Man coming on the clouds of heaven with power and great glory [in brilliancy and splendor]. And He will send out His angels with a loud trumpet call, and they will gather His elect (His chosen ones) from the four winds, [even] from one end of the universe to the other.

There will be signs everywhere, and if you take heed you will not be left behind. But if you do not, you will be as the goats—separated from the sheep. God wants us to be ready for His coming; and He gives us many signs that we should look for and recognize. If we ignore them and proceed with our own things, then we not only do an injustice to ourselves, we will also cause Him to put us aside and cause us to be without Him. However, if we will do what He says, not only will we be in tune with God; we will also be able to live with Him.

CHAPTER 10
THE REASON CHRIST CAME

The reason Christ came to earth in the form of a man was to cleanse us from our sins and to reconcile us back to God. In the Old Testament the people had to present a lamb without spot, blemish, or wrinkles and offer a blood sacrifice to God each year for their sins. In the New Testament we no longer have to offer a lamb without spot, blemish or wrinkles because God provided Himself as the ultimate sacrifice. God Himself offered up Jesus Christ His Only begotten Son as a one-time ultimate sacrifice without spot, without blemish, and without wrinkles as a sweet smelling savor and it's not just for one year but it's for a lifetime. Yes, He was born just to die. He died for you and for me.

John 3:16 states:

> *For God so greatly loved and dearly prized the world that He [even] gave up His only begotten (unique) son, so that whoever believes in (trust in, clings to, relies on) him shall not perish (come to destruction, be lost) but have eternal (everlasting) life.*

He loves you and me so much that it pleased God to bruise His own Son according to Isaiah 53:10. Now this is what took place because of the willingness to the Father.

John 18:1-9 states:

> *Having said these things, Jesus went out with His disciples beyond (across) the winter torrent of the Kidron [in the ravine]. There was a garden there, which He and His disciples entered. And Judas, who was betraying Him and delivering Him up, also knew the place, because Jesus had often retired there with His disciples. So Judas, obtaining and taking*

*charge of the band of soldiers and some guards (attendant) of
the high priest and Pharisees, came there with lanterns and
torches and weapons. Then Jesus, knowing all that was about
to befall Him, went out to them and said; whom are you
seeking? [Whom do you want?]. They answered Him, Jesus
the Nazarene. Jesus said to them, I am He. Judas who was
betraying Him was also standing with them. When Jesus said
to them, I am He; they went backwards (drew back, lurched
backward) and fell to the ground. Then again He asked them,
whom are you seeking? And they said Jesus the Nazarene. Jesus
answered; I told you that I am He. So if you want me [if t is
only I for whom you are looking], let these men go their way.
Thus what He said was fulfilled and verified, of those whom
You have given Me, I have not lost even one.*

This was the night they came and arrested Jesus and tried to
accuse Him of saying and doing things. They said what He did
was wrong because He called Himself the Son of God. It was
blasphemy in those days to say that you were like God or even to
consider yourself His son. However, Jesus could not lie because
He was the Son of God and God in the flesh.

Matthew 27:27-31 states:

*Then the governor's soldiers took Jesus into the palace, and they
gathered the whole battalion about Him. And they striped
off His clothes and put a scarlet robe (a garment of dignity
and office worn by Roman officers of rank) upon Him. And
weaving a crown of thorns, they put it on His head and put a
reed (staff) in His right hand. And kneeling before Him, they
made sport of Him, saying hail (greetings, good health to you,
long life to you), King of the Jews. And they spat on Him, and
took the reed (staff) and struck Him on the head. And when
they finished making sport of Him, they stripped Him of the
robe and put His own garments on Him and led Him away
to be crucified.*

The death of Jesus, according to the gospels is, that

1. He was beaten mercilessly and they nailed Him to the cross His hands and His feet.
2. He was crucified in a place called Calvary.
3. They gave Him vinegar to drink because He was thirsty from hanging there for six hours.
4. The people made fun of Him.
5. The veil of the temple was rent.
6. He rose from the dead the third day.

Matthew 27:45-54 states:

Now from the sixth hour (noon) there was darkness over all the land until the ninth hour (three o'clock). And about the ninth hour Jesus cried with a loud voice, Eli, Eli, lama sabachthani?—that is, My God, My God, why have you abandoned me [leaving Me helpless, forsaking and failing Me in My need]? And some of the bystanders, when they heard it, said, this man is calling for Elijah! And one of them immediately ran and took a sponge, soaked it with vinegar (a sour wine), and put it on a reed (staff), and was about to give it to Him to drink. But others said, wait, let us see whether Elijah will come to save Him from death. And Jesus cried again with a loud voice and gave up His spirit. And at once the curtain of the sanctuary of the temple was torn in two from top to bottom; the earth shook and the rocks were split. The tombs were opened and many bodies of the saints who had fallen asleep in death were raised [to life]; and coming out of the tombs after His resurrection, they went into the holy city and appeared to many people. When the centurion and those who were with him keeping watch over Jesus observed the earthquake and all that was happening, they were terribly frightened and filled with awe, and said, truly this was God's Son.

The people standing around finally believed that Jesus was the One when they saw everything that was done. God showed up and cause the people to recognize who Jesus really was. The veil of the temple ripped on its own, which was amazing in and of itself.

He was hung between two thieves, one on the right the other on the left. The one on the left said, "If you be the Son of God take Yourself and us off the cross." The one on the right said, "This man has done no wrong." He turns to Jesus and says, "Remember me when You come into Your kingdom;" and Jesus said, "Today you shall be with Me in paradise."

Luke 23:39-43 states:

> *One of the criminals who were suspended kept up a railing at Him, saying, are you not the Christ (the Messiah)? Rescue yourself and us [from death]! But the other one reproved him; do you not even fear God, seeing you yourself are under the same sentence of condemnation and suffering the same penalty? And we indeed suffer it justly, receiving the due reward of our actions; but this Man has done nothing out of the way [nothing strange or eccentric or perverse or unreasonable]. Then he said to Jesus, Lord; remember me when you come in Your kingly glory! And He answered him, truly I tell you, today you shall be with Me in paradise.*

Even the thief on the right believed in Jesus and he was at the point of death. That goes to show that if you are at the point of death and you call on Him, He will forgive you. All you have to do is call on Him. Both men had the same opportunity but only one took advantage of it and chose to believe even at the point of death. Do not waste the opportunity that you have been given.

Do not be like the thief on the left, he lost his chance of heaven. Don't lose yours.

Towards the end before Jesus died He said, "Father, forgive them, for they know not what they do." Would that be your prayer if someone had offended you? It will be once you have a relationship with Jesus. He transforms you to be like Him. He also said, "It is finished." What He came to do was done, and then He died. The soldiers came and broke the two thieves' legs because they were yet alive and when they came to Jesus and found that He was dead already they pierced Him in the side where blood and water poured out.

John 19:30-37 states:

> *When Jesus had received the sour wine, He said, it is finished! And He bowed His head and give up His spirit. Since it was the day of preparation, in order to prevent the bodies from hanging on the cross on the Sabbath-for that Sabbath was a very solemn and important one-the Jews requested Pilate to have the legs broken and the bodies taken away. So the soldiers came and broke the legs of the first one, and of the other who had been crucified with Him. But when they came to Jesus and they saw that He was already dead, they did not break His legs, but one of the soldiers pierced His side with a spear, and immediately blood and water came (flowing) out, and he who saw it (the eyewitness) gives this evidence, and his testimony is true; and he knows that he tells the truth, that you may believe also. For these things took place, that the scripture might be fulfilled (verified, carried out), not one of His bones shall be broken; and again another scripture says, they shall look on Him Whom they have pierced.*

They did all manner of things to Him and He did not say a word. He just let them have their way with Him. These things Jesus suffered for us so that we can be reconciled to God and also to show us how much He loves us. Because of this, we owe Him our lives.

When they took Him down from the cross, Joseph asked to have His body and they wrapped Him as it was their custom, and they placed Him in a borrowed tomb.

Matthew 27:57:60 states:

> *When it was evening there came a rich man from Arimathea, named Joseph, who also was a disciple of Jesus. He went to Pilate and asked for the body of Jesus, and Pilate ordered that it be given to him, and Joseph took the body and rolled it up in clean linen cloth used for swathing dead bodies and laid it in his own fresh (undefiled) tomb, which he had hewn in the rock; and he rolled a big boulder over the door of the tomb and went away.*

Many followers of Jesus were in hiding for fear of the Jews; Joseph was one of them, but he was bold enough to ask Pilate for the body of Jesus and gave Him his own tomb because they did not actually have one on hand for Him. God always makes away.

Although Jesus was dead, the priests and the Pharisees were still afraid of Him. They wanted to make sure that the tomb was secure and no one could take the body of Jesus, claiming that He was risen. So they asked for soldiers to keep watch.

Matthew 27:62-66 states:

> *The next day, that is, the day after the day of preparation [for the Sabbath], the chief priests and the Pharisees assembled before Pilate and said, sir, we have such remembered how that vagabond imposter said while He was yet alive, after*

three days I will rise again. Therefore give an order to have the tomb made secure and safeguarded until the third day, for fear that His disciples will come and steal Him away and tell the people that He has risen from the dead, and the last deception and fraud will be worse than the first. Pilate said to them, you have a guard [of soldiers; take them and] go, make it as secure as you can. So they went off and made the tomb secure by sealing the boulder, a guard of soldiers being with them and remaining to watch.

They took as many soldiers as they could to make sure no one actually came to take the body because He was to be raised the third day according to what Jesus had told them.

So God in His infinite wisdom made them safeguard the tomb so that they could actually be witnesses of His resurrection. God loves to show off and He would have wanted people to see not only His death but to see somewhat of His resurrection also.

Matthew 28:1-7 states:

Now after the Sabbath, near dawn of the first day of the week, Mary of Magdala and the other Mary went to take a look at the tomb; and behold there was a great earthquake, for an angel of the Lord descended from heaven and came and rolled the boulder back and sat upon it. His appearance was like lightening, and his garment was white as snow. And those keeping guard were so frightened at the sight of him that they were agitated and they trembled and became like dead men, but the angel said to the women, Do not be alarmed and frightened, for I know that you are looking for Jesus, who was crucified. He is not here; He has risen, as He said [He would do]. Come see the place where He lay. Then go quickly and tell His disciples, He has risen from the dead, and behold, I have told you.

The stone was rolled away in order for the people to see that He was not there, that He had already been raised and the tomb was empty. He got out with the doors still intact because He did not need to use a door anymore. He was man no more. At least the guards were there to be witnesses to the miracle.

THE BRIBING OF THE SOLDIERS

The guards told the priest what had happened and they gave them money to lie because they did not want to believe that that was what really happened.

Matthew 28:11-15 states:

> *While they were on their way, behold, some of the guards went into the city and reported to the chief priests everything that had occurred. And when they [the chief priests] had gathered with the elders and had consulted together, they gave a sufficient sum of money to the solders, and said, tell people, His disciples came at night and stole Him away while we were sleeping and if the governor hears of it, we will appease him and make you safe and free from trouble and care. So they took the money and do as they were instructed; and this story had been current among the Jews to the present day.*

The elders were so afraid; they wanted to make sure nothing that Jesus had said would come to pass. So they took precautions and measures that these things would not come to fruition so they prepared themselves for it. They did not know that no matter what they tried to do or how much they tried to stop Jesus from coming out of the grave, they never could stop what God has purposed to do.

1. They were afraid and wanted to make sure He did not raise from the dead
2. They were afraid and wanted as many soldiers to keep guard.
3. They were afraid that what Jesus said might actually come to pass.
4. They were afraid that what the soldiers actually witnessed was really true.
5. They give the soldiers money not to tell anyone what they had seen.

People would rather believe a lie than the truth. The truth sounds too far fetched and impossible while the lie seems more reasonable and possible. The difference is that the soldiers could not deny what had really happened in their hearts no matter how many lies they spoke.

THE GREAT COMMISSION

The eleven disciples (Judas had killed himself because he felt guilty for betraying innocent blood) went away into Galilee into the mountain where Jesus had appointed them to meet Him. Jesus came and spoke unto them telling them what He wanted them to do.

Matthew 28:16-20 states:

Now the eleven disciples went to Galilee, to the mountain to which Jesus had directed and made appointment with them. And when they saw Him they fell down and worshipped Him; but some doubted. Jesus approached, and breaking the silence, said to them, all authority (all power of rule) in heaven and on earth had been given Me. Go then and make disciples of all the nations, baptizing them in the Name of the Father and of the Son and of the Holy Spirit. Teaching them to observe everything that I have commanded you, and behold, I am with you all the days (perpetually, uniformly, and on every occasion), to the [very] close and consummation of the age. Amen (so let it be).

The disciples were told,

1. To meet Jesus in a place that He had designated.
2. To go and teach all over the nation.
3. To feed His Sheep (the adults).
4. To feed His Lambs (the children).
5. To baptize in the name of the Father, Son, and Holy Spirit.

Jesus wants us all to be baptized and to be witnesses for Him. He wants us to preach His word and He has already taught us what we should repeat to others so they too can come to Him. So Jesus died, rose again on the third day, and is now sitting at the right hand of God the Father. He gave us a command and that is to teach all nations about Him and what He has done for us. While He was on earth, He healed the sick. He raised the dead. He caused the blind to see. He caused the lame to walk. He caused the deaf to hear. He cast out demons and He even walked on water. It's all in the bible. Everything you want to know is in the bible. You have to be able to know what it says to be able to do what you need to do and at the right time that you need it done. The bible has love stories, war stories, hate and betrayal, how to live right, also what to do and what not to do, stories that make you laugh, stories that make you cry, stories that even have a twist, stories that make you think, stories that make you wonder how they could do what they did. It's all in the book. Read it some time and you will be intrigued. It's all true and it all pertains to your life and to life in general. If you want to live you must stay in the Word. If you want to be successful you must stay in the word.

If you want to overcome you must stay in the word. If you want to be like Jesus you must stay in the word. You have to stay in the word and you will be what God wants you to be. It is a vital part of your life to remain in God's word and it will not only change your life it will make your life better as you seek to live like God intend. It will also help you to raise your children right, to stay married and to be successful.

You must eat, sleep, think on, meditate on, dream of and live the word. It's your life; what do you have to lose? All you have to lose are your problems, your trials, your frustrations, your anxiety, and everything else that's not working in your life. When you meditate in the word you will get to know the One who died for you. You will get to know the creator of everything and He will be your Father and you will be His sons and daughters.

CHAPTER 11
A PRICE PAID

Do you know that Jesus loves you? Well, He does. Is your soul worth going to hell? Are you aware that a price was paid for your soul? Do you know what you're worth? Well, because you're worthwhile to God, He has paid a price to save you. A price that cost Him everything and which cost you nothing. A price that even if you tried to pay you could not, no matter how much money you may have, or how good you are, or even how much you give of your time volunteering.

He paid a dept that He did not owe and we owe a dept that we could never ever pay. It cost God everything to set us free from sin and death. It cost God His best and we do not even appreciate what He has done for us. We're still the same old way; we live anyway we want, with not as much as a consideration of what He has done.

1. Yes, it cost something for your salvation.
2. Yes, it cost something for you to get free from drugs.
3. Yes, it cost something for you to be healed.
4. Yes, it cost something for you to be set free from sin and death.
5. Yes, it cost something for you to live an abundant life.

Yes, it cost something. We could not ever understand why He would give His all for us. His love is so much towards us that He would have done anything even giving His own life for us because we are precious to Him.

Romans 5:8 states: *But God shows and clearly proves His [own] love for us by the fact that while we were still sinners, Christ (the Messiah, the Anointed One) died for us.*

Yet it cost you nothing. All you have to do is come to Jesus. To give your life to Him and when you do, it shows your appreciation for what it cost Him. For this reason came He into the world. My friend, God has not forgotten you. He knows where you are and He will meet you at the point of your need. He will meet you exactly where you are.

GOD HAS DONE HIS PART

God has already done His part, your part is to move towards Him then He will, in turn, move toward you. His hands are stretched out wide waiting for you to enter. He wants to hold you, to comfort and soothe you. He promises never to leave you nor forsake you. If you're a backslider, you may have thought God had abandoned you. You thought that the thing you might have done caused Him to turn away from you; so you just kept on doing what you were doing and falling deeper and deeper into sin. God hates sin. He turns His back and His face from sin. God does not and never will hate you. He hates what you've done, and are doing, but He does not hate you. Maybe you've prayed and God never answered your prayer. He may not have answered because:

1. Maybe what you were praying for may not be yours.
2. Maybe it may not have been the correct timing.
3. Maybe it might not have been God's best for your life.
4. Maybe you were not ready to receive what you asked for.

Without knowing the reason why God never answered you; you became frustrated and thought that God did not like you, so you gave up. Walking with God takes patience and endurance. I, too, had turned my back on God because I thought He had abandoned me just when I needed Him the most, and I lived many years bitter not better. When I reaccepted Him as Lord and

Savior of my life; I realized that I had left Him, He did not leave me. He was always there looking out for me and looking after me. I did not wait long enough to get the correct answer. I bailed out because I thought He never came through with the thing I had asked Him to do. Many years later I found out that that thing I was asking God for is what I thought I wanted at that time, but came to find out that I never really wanted or needed that thing after all. Now I thank God all the time that He never gave me that thing which I had asked for so long ago, and I came out better, stronger, smarter and wiser than I would have been had I not gone through what I did. So don't get upset or angry with God because things did not happen for you. He knows you better than you know yourself. He also knows what's best for you, so be patient and wait, because He will never fail you. He will give you what is best for you and nothing that will harm you.

UNFORGIVENESS

I had a friend who once told me that he had prayed to God for something and he believed and trusted God and God never answered his prayer. He was very bitter towards God and went on with his life full of hate knowing that there was a God, but like the children of Israel who turned their backs on God and worshipped idols, my friend was now this way. He would rather believe in a false god than believe in the true and living God. In other words, he renounced God and started worshiping His creations and calling on the beings that were out there. Later on in life when I became a Christian I saw my friend again. He was now thirty years old and had cancer of the eye. The eye was bulging out of his head and was full of pus. I asked him what happened and he told me that his girlfriend, when she was pregnant with his child had cancer, which was taking a toll on her. So he wanted her to have some kind of comfort. He prayed to some being out there for them to take the cancer from her and give it to him instead.

Now that he has the cancer, his girlfriend, of course, still had it too.

There are a lot of evil spirits out there and once you pray to some being, trust me, the devil will answer. I ask him why did he not prayed to God and ask for His help in time of need, He would most certainly help you. With an attitude, he said that he was never talking to God again and that he'd rather die before he asked God for anything, how he no longer believed in Him, and he would never pray to Him. Now that shocks me to see that someone whom I once knew and who once loved, trusted, relied on and believed in God would say such things about God. I could not understand that. I spoke to him regarding salvation but he would not accept. You see, that's bitterness taken too far. He could not forgive God. If he had stopped to regurgitate what it was that he was asking God for; he would have realized that it was not what God had wanted in his life at that time. He did not stick around long enough to find out what God had to say. I'm sure he did not know how to do that because when he asked God for that thing, he was very young. He did not get what he wanted so he resorted to childish attitude.

You could remember when you were a child and you're playing with your friend or friends and one did something to you and you said, "I'm not talking to you anymore." But less than five minutes later you and that friend are the best of friends playing again? I remember many a day when my cousin (whom I consider my sister) and I used to play and fall out all the time and I would stop talking to her (I was very stubborn), but she would always come to me and ask me to talk to her and I always would. Well, he stopped talking to God and they never became friends again.

Although God was always asking him to talk to Him, he never could, or never wanted to. I know this because God had told me to go and see him the night before he died. So God was always waiting for him to come back, always beckoning him, but he never did. Even at the point of death God waited for him; wanting him to talk to Him, sending someone to speak to him; that's how much God loved him. Although everything that he did and all of the idol worship, God still loved him and wanted to save his soul. My friend took it too far, opening doors for demonic activities in his life. We spoke a little about accepting Jesus and what Jesus did for him, but he only laughed and said, "Never." He died one month later. Don't let that happen to you. Don't let bitterness fill your heart. God is a loving, caring, good and forgiving God. He wants what's best for you. Don't harbor bitterness towards God; release it.

You may be asking, "How do you know God was there beckoning him to come back to Him?" Well, the night before he died God told me to visit him. God knew that he was going to die without Christ and wanted to give him another opportunity, another chance to get his life right. God loved him too much to see him going to hell and not do something about it.

Unforgiveness makes your heart hard. It makes you mean and bitter towards people. It makes you do the same things that were done to you. It makes you turn from God, and it makes you hate with a passion.

Do not harbor unforgiveness in your heart; it will only tear you apart and it will bring you down. You will make yourself miserable and others around you will be miserable, too. This is a disease that sits in your heart and is very hard to get rid of; and you will find that you will not only look mean and old but you will feel empty and unfulfilled. God wants us to forgive and to release whatever it is that is bothering us and if we want to be free we must relinquish all the hatred and bitterness that we feel inside.

GOD HONORS HIS WORD

God's word is true. He honors His word above His name and His name is most powerful. Whatever we ask in His name He gives us once it's according to His will for our lives. At His name, demons are cast out. At His name, Alzheimer's has to go. At His name, infirmities have to go. At His name, Down's syndrome has to go. At His name, sickness has to bow. At His name, every other name has to bow, Cancer, Tumors, Aids, STD's, Diabetes and even Obesities. Also at His name, every knee shall bow.

See how powerful His name is? Yet He honors His word above His name. Don't be too quick to give up on God all because He did not answer what you were asking Him for. He knows what's best for you. He is also building your character and allowing you to draw closer to Him. Yea, you may say, I know all of that, and I was even doing all of that, but yet I lost my home, yet I lost my car, yet I lost my friends, yet my spouse still left me, yet I still lost my job. The list may go on and on and you cannot see why God will allow all these negative things to happen to you. My children are acting up, or my child is in prison and you're asking, where is God in all this? Well, He's right there beside you feeling your pain. Instead of complaining and questioning God just talk to Him,

1. What am I to learn from this?
2. What am I supposed to get out of this?
3. Help me to learn what You want me to learn from this.
4. Help me to do what You want me to do.
5. Help me to implement it where I'm productive.

The more you complain, you tie God's hand to do anything for you and you allow the enemy to step in and cause a rift between you and God. The devil likes nothing better than for you to be away from God. I know that's not easy to do and not what you want to hear, but it is the truth. He will let you see and know what you should get out of that situation whatever it may be. Just know that He will bring you out. This too shall pass. Don't let complaints tie the hand of God in your life.

Numbers 11:4-6 states:

> *And the mixed multitude among them [the rabble who followed Israel from Egypt] began to lust greatly [for familiar and dainty food], and the Israelites wept again and said, who will give us meat to eat? We remember the fish we ate freely in Egypt and without cost, the cucumbers, melons, leeks, onions, and garlic. But now our soul (our strength) is dried up; there is nothing at all [in the way of food] to be seen but this manna.*

The children of Israel complained because they remembered everything they used to have in Egypt. They were complaining that they were no longer getting those things to eat that they were accustoming to.

Verses 18-20 state:

> *And say to the people, consecrate yourselves for tomorrow, and you shall eat meat; for you have wept in the ear of the Lord, saying, who will give us meat to eat? For it was well with us in Egypt. Therefore the Lord will give you meat, and you shall eat. You shall not eat one day, or two, or five, or ten, or twenty days. But a whole month-until [you are satiated and vomit it up violently and] it comes out at your nostrils and is disgusting to you-because you have rejected and despised the Lord who is among you, and have wept before Him, saying, why did we come out of Egypt?*

God was going to give them the things that they wanted but He was not pleased with them. Be careful what you're asking God to do because if it is not in His will and you keep on asking, He might just give it to you and cause you pain afterwards.

Verse 31-33 state:

> *And there went forth a wind from the Lord and brought quails from the sea, and let them fall [so they flew low] beside the camp, about a days journey on this side and on the other side, all around the camp, about two cubits above the ground. And the people rose all that day and all night and all the next day and caught and gathered the quails. He who gathered least gathered ten homers; and they spread them out for themselves round about the camp [to cure them by drying]. While the meat was yet between their teeth, before it was consumed, the anger of the Lord was kindled against the people, and the Lord smote them with a very great plague.*

God caused a plague to come upon them because they were not content with where they were and so they complained just to get what they wanted and caused wrath and punishment upon themselves.

The situation will get worse before it gets better, but if you praise God and give Him glory no matter the situation; He will bring you out, and He will get all the glory. The longer you take to praise Him the longer you get to stay in your situation. Just thank Him knowing that He will bring you out. Knowing that weeping may endure for a night, but joy will come in the morning. He loves you and everything pertaining to you. Sometimes you have to go through things in order to grow.

My bishop, Noel Jones spoke on growing up one Sunday; he made a point of asking how you know you are grown. It's because if you can go through all those horrific things and you are still praising God, then you know that you have grown. The thing or things (because more times than not, we are going through more that one thing at a time) that you are going through become your testimony; you are then better equipped to handle the next challenge and be able to reach out to someone who is going through that same thing that you went through.

You can say to them with ease how you handled that situation and that they should handle it this way because you at first did not know how to handle it; but now I do, and it would help you come out faster if you do it this way. Remember, what you are going through is not just for you but for whom you can be a blessing to. God knows our needs. He knows you inside out. Just remember that trouble doesn't last always, strong people do. It makes a difference what you do when trouble comes. So when the problems do come (and they will), just praise God instead of looking at your circumstances and what you have or what you do not have. Praise Him anyways because praising God will bring you out faster. Moping around complaining will keep you in the fire that much longer.

THE SINNER'S PRAYER

Jesus asked in Matthew chapter 16:26 *What shall a man profit if he gains the whole world and lose his own soul or what shall a man give in exchange for his soul?* This is a question that we take for granted. We do not realize that our souls will live on in eternity and we do not dwell on or think about it in a serious manner. What is more important than your soul?

There are people who offer up their first born for riches and fame and/or even their own souls and when the time comes for the reaper to harvest their souls then they realize what they have done and want to change, but there are no take-backs and he (the devil) will come for your soul. You cannot play with the devil and do not expect to be burned. You may not take it seriously, but it's no joke. Nothing is worth losing your soul over because what you're giving up is more valuable than what you're getting back.

God created you and the only one that should have your soul is God because it belongs to Him in the first place. It is and was He that has made us and gives to us what we have and it all still belongs to Him. We should not be so ungrateful and try to bargain with the enemy. God was the One that made you and created you and gave you all your talents and abilities. He is the One that enhances those abilities. People are so desperate that they turn to something that cannot really help them but hinders them.

Romans 8:28-31 states:

> *We are assured and know that [God being a partner in their labor] all things work together and are [fitting into a plan] for good to and for those who love God and are called according to [His] design and purpose. For those whom He foreknew [of whom He was aware and loved beforehand], He also destined from the beginning [foreordaining them] to be molded into the image of His Son [and share inwardly His likeness], that He might become the firstborn among many brethren. And those whom He thus foreordained, He also called; and those whom He called, He also justified (acquitted, made righteous, putting them into right standing with Himself). And those whom He justified, He also glorified [raising them to a heavenly dignity and condition or state of being]. What then shall we say to [all] this? If God is for us, who [can be] against us? [who can be our foe, if God is on our side?]*

Those of you who would like to accept Jesus Christ as Lord and Savior of your life, and you are willing to give up your old ways and habits and serve Jesus. Even those of you who have backslidden and would like to rededicate your life to God, then you can also repeat the sinner's prayer.

1 John 1:9 states:

If we [freely] admit that we have sinned and confess our sins, He is faithful and just (true to His own nature and promises) and will forgive our sins [dismiss our lawlessness] and [continuously] cleanse us from all unrighteousness [everything not in conformity to His will in purpose, thought, and action].

Once you've made a confession, He promises that He will forgive you, but you first have to do something and then He will do something.

Romans 10:9 states:

Because if you acknowledge and confess with your lips that Jesus is Lord and in your heart believe (adhere to, trust in, and rely on the truth) that God raised Him from the dead, you will be saved. You have to believe with all your heart and He will save you.

Romans 10:13 states: *For anyone who calls upon the name of the Lord [invoking Him as Lord] will be saved.*

He said just to call on His name and He will do it for you.

Romans 6:23 states: *For the wages which sin pays is death, but the [bountiful] free gift of God is eternal life through (in union with) Jesus Christ our Lord.*

It is a free gift from God; so all you have to do now is to repeat the sinner's prayer. It's your first step to becoming a born again believer (Christian).

> Father, I come to You a sinner. Please come into my heart and forgive me of all my sins. I believe that Your Son Jesus died, shed His blood for me, and rose again from the grave on the third day so that I can live. Wash me in Your precious blood and make me as white as snow. I renounce Satan and put him under my feet. Make me a new creature and write my name in the Lamb's Book Of Life. I thank You for loving me, in Jesus name, Amen.

That was not so bad. Was it?

2Corinthians 5:17 states:

> *Therefore if any person is [in grafted] in Christ (the Messiah) he is a new creation (a new creature altogether); the old [previous moral and spiritual condition] has passed away. Behold the fresh and new has come.*

You are no longer a sinner, but a saint of God. You are a child of God. The whole hosts of angels are rejoicing over you because you have given Christ your life and have decided to come in, or back into the sheepfold. You may stumble at times but that does not mean that God does not love you any more; you just pick yourself up, ask God to forgive you, and keep on going.

Do not keep blaming yourself for what happened and do not keep wondering if God will ever forgive you. He will forgive you once you ask His forgiveness. Those of you who have children would understand parents' love for their children. If your children did something wrong, would you hate them? No. You may hate what they did, but you could never hate your children, and when they come to you and ask your forgiveness, don't you forgive them right away without punishing them severely? Well, God is very much like that, He is our parent and He loves us no matter what. Yes, He hates sin very much, but He would never hate you. So just ask God to forgive you of all your shortcomings and try not to do that thing again and ask Him to help you to overcome your struggles.

YOU MUST FELLOWSHIP

Now if you prayed this prayer and really meant it with all your heart then you are no longer that same person. God has sent His Holy Spirit to now live within you; you no longer do the things you used to do, because old things are passed away and behold all things have become new. Well, this does not mean that you are perfect and can do no wrong. The difference is, when you want to do wrong you will try your best with the help of the Holy Spirit to do the right things. If you happen to do something wrong, the Holy Spirit will convict you of your wrong doings. Do not ignore this conviction. Repent right away.

You now need to find yourself a church where you can become a member. The pastor would be the one God has put in place to watch over your soul. That means that he or she will pray to God for you and will be your covering. They can pray for you individually yes, but they really pray corporately for their members that God has placed under them. You go to church because,

1. You need to hear the word of God.
2. You need to have someone watching over your soul.
3. You need to be able to grow from carnality to spirituality.

4. You need to be able to meet with your other family in Christ.

You need to fellowship with your other brothers and sisters in Christ Jesus. Also, make sure you are baptized with water. If you need love, joy, peace, happiness, only God can give them to you. You need to build your relationship with Jesus. In order to do so, you have to read your bible every day to see how He wants you to live. You also need to pray everyday starting with at least fifteen minutes a day and work your way up to at least one hour a day, just you and Him, no interruptions.

There's a saying, "little prayer-little power, much prayer-much power." How much power do you want? The more you do these things the stronger your faith becomes and the more you will be open to hear from God. Get in a good bible-based church and go as often as you can. Be eager to learn so you can grow. Make an effort to go because your growth and development depend on it.

Remember if you slip and fall, Romans 8:1 states: *Therefore, [there is] now no condemnation (no adjudging guilt of wrong) for those who are in Christ Jesus, who live [and] walk not after the dictates of the flesh, but after the dictates of the spirit.*

So if you walk after the spirit, you will not fulfill the lust of the flesh and God will not condemn you. He will forgive you once you ask forgiveness of Him.

TROUBLE WILL COME

Now, being a Christian does not mean that the devil will leave you alone. The devil will try you; put obstacles in your way and sometimes you might feel that you are not saved, but keep on doing what God says to do. Trouble will come but it will not last.

It may seem that it is lasting a very long time, but keep the faith. Don't lose hope and God will bring you out.

1Peter 4:12-14 states:

> *Beloved, do not be amazed and bewildered at the fiery ordeal which is taking place to test your quality, as though something strange (unusual and alien to you and your position) were befalling you. But insofar as you are sharing Christ's sufferings, rejoice, so that when His glory [full of radiance and splendor] is revealed, you may also rejoice with triumph [exultantly]. If you are censured and suffer abuse [because you bear] the name of Christ, blessed [are you-happy, fortunate, to be envied, with life-joy, and satisfaction in God's favor and salvation, regardless of you outward condition], because the Spirit of glory, the Spirit of God, is resting upon you. On their part He is blasphemed, but on your part He is glorified.*

When you get saved, there are some things that you will have to go through. You will feel that all hell has broken loose in your life. It will be as though nothing is going right in your life and you will feel like God has made a fool of you. Do not let what you see cause you to turn back. Just keep the faith. You may see sometimes that your finance is low; you can't seem to make ends meet; you can't afford to pay your rent; you got evicted; your car gets repossessed and your furniture too; your child just went to jail; your spouse just walked out on you or a family member that's close to you just died. You cannot understand why it was after you got saved that now these things are happening to you and you want to give up, but God is still with you. Although it does not look like it, He will always be there for you. The devil went to God after losing you and God is allowing him to take his best shot at you to show him (the devil) that you will still love and serve God no matter what you go through. Don't let your circumstances get you down. Just know that you are blessed to be a partaker of Jesus' suffering.

1 Peter 4:14 states: *But if [one is ill—treated and suffers] as a Christian [which he is contemptuously called], let him not be ashamed, but give glory to God that he is [deemed worthy to suffer] in this name.*

Stay in the wilderness until it is time to come out and you will get back double what the enemy has taken from you. God is still next to you and you will hear Him after a while. The hedge will be built back around you again; do not lose hope. Do not complain; but be faithful in what you do, and God will bring you out with a mighty hand.

1 Peter 1:7 states:

> So that [the genuineness] of your faith may be tested [your faith] which is infinitely more precious than the perishable gold which is tested and purified by fire. [This proving of your faith is intended] to redound to [your] praise and glory and honor when Jesus Christ (the messiah, the Anointing One) is reviled.

He is trying to see how much you love Him and how faithful you will be. He's counting on you not to give up. You will see that it is for your good: to build you up and for you to become what He has destined for you to become.

CHAPTER 12
A PRICE TO PAY

What are you willing to pay for your soul? There is a price to pay and although Jesus paid the ultimate price, there's still one that you have to pay. Salvation is free. There's no charge to come to Christ but yet it cost you something. It cost you your time, your old ways, and you must die to self.

TIME

Your time because it takes time out of your busy schedule to build a relationship with Christ. You just cannot accept Him as Lord and Savior of your life and don't expect to spend quality time with Him. A relationship just does not work on its own. It takes quality time.

1. It takes time in prayer and meditation.
2. It takes time in reading your word.
3. It takes time in going to church.
4. It takes time in ministering to others.
5. It takes time making sure that you are doing what God says and wants for you.

No matter what you try to do or say, you cannot get around spending time with God if you want to be closer or even have a closer walk with Him. If you want what He's got for you, you have to put your time in. You need to take every opportunity to spend with Him. You need to always have Him on your mind and in your heart. Do not put anyone in the place where God is supposed to be and do not let anyone take over your heart and you forget about God because it is only God who can and will be there when all others have forsaken you.

YOUR OLD WAYS

Your old ways because the places you used to go and accustomed to you can no longer visit. Places like the clubs, the bars, or the strip joint. You know where you often visit. Everybody knows your name there. Sometimes you will get the urge to go and sometimes you may even slip up and go, but you must know that you are a work in progress. Now, this does not give you the license to sin, but if and when you do there is nothing wrong with you. You are simply in a process of getting over it. Do not presumptuously sin, because God will punish.

2 Corinthians 6:17 states: *So, come out from among [unbelievers], and separate (sever) yourselves from them, says the Lord, and touch not [any] unclean thing; then I will receive you kindly and treat you with favor.*

When you do not touch the unclean things:

1. God will receive you unto Himself.
2. God will give you favor.
3. God will give you your heart's desires.
4. God will protect you from harm.
5. God will always be there helping you each step of the way.

Things like cigarettes, smoking crack, pot, drugs, alcohol and such like manner you have to stay away from. I know that it will be hard, but you have to fight the cravings and God will help you to overcome.

DIE TO SELF

Die to self because things of the flesh that you did such as anger, hate, meanness, cursing, lying, fornicating, fussing, fighting, and such like have to be put away.

Luke 9:23 states:

> *And He said to all, if any person wills to come after Me, let him deny himself [disown himself, forget, lose sight of himself and his own interests, refuse and give up himself] and take up his cross daily and follow Me [cleave steadfastly to Me, conform wholly to My example in living and, if need be, in dying also].*

You must forget that you actually exist and it's now Christ living in you. You are no longer you and you must live like you belong to someone. You have to,

1. Forget the things you want to do.
2. You have to remember that you belong to God.
3. You have to cleave to God.
4. You have to fellowship with God.
5. You have to give yourself completely to God.

Luke 14:26 states:

> *If any one comes to Me and does not hate his [own] father and mother [in the sense of indifference to or relative disregard for them in comparison with his attitude towards God] and [likewise] his wife and children and brothers and sisters and even his own life also-he cannot be My disciple.*

In order to come to God you have to do the things that you find really difficult to do; but for you to get God you have to give up the things you love the most.

1. Give up your family.
   a. Your husband and wife.
   b. Your sons and your daughters.
   c. Your sisters and your brothers.
   d. Your mothers and your fathers.
2. Give up your friends.
3. Give up your job.
4. Give up material things.
   a. Such as your money.
   b. Such as your cars.
   c. Such as your houses.
   d. Such as your lands.

You have to give up anything and everything that your heart's desire or that you have or possess. When those things are put away God give you back some things that are much better. He gives you back love, peace, longsuffering, patience, gentleness, goodness, faith, meekness, and temperance. These things are to build you up and not tear you down. Things that build Christ-like character that you can use and be a blessing to others. Only these things can get you into heaven.

JESUS, YOUR TICKET TO HEAVEN

Jesus is your ticket to heaven yes, but you can lose your ticket if these character traits are not in you. Things such as meanness and other like characters will cause you to lose your ticket to heaven and replace it with a one-way ticket to hell. So what is your part in all this? Your part is simply to know that you are in the faith and make sure that you stay there. You stay there by, after accepting Jesus you keep all the commandments.

The first commandment is for us to love God with everything that we are and everything that we have. The one that says to honor your parents is one with a promise. God says if we do honor our parents we would live long and prosperous lives. So remember to treat your parents right.

Don't forget that you have to love God above and beyond anyone or anything and to love your neighbors as yourself. Why? It's because if you will love Him the way He tells you to love Him, you will automatically love your neighbors as yourself and you will not want to hurt them. You will not want to kill anyone, steal from anyone or even do anything that displeases God. Love will not only cover a multitude of sin, but true love will never fail.

TRUE LOVE

True and genuine love will always protect and care for the person. The love you have for God will determine the way in which you will treat others. I know if I ask if you love God, you will say yes; however, loving God is much more than saying "I love you." You can say, "I love you" to your spouse and to a loved one and do not even mean that. I know because I did it all the time and never meant a word of it.

1John 4:16 states:

> *And we know (understand, recognize, are conscious of, by observation and by experience) and believe (adhere to and put faith in and rely on) the love God cherishes for us. God is love, and he who dwells and continues in love dwells and continues in God, and God dwells and continues in him.*

If you dwell in God and continue in Him,

1. Then the love of God will show through you.
2. Then the love that is in you will flow to others.
   a. You will give.
   b. You will help.
   c. You will lend.
   d. You will serve.
3. Then you will be willing to go out of your way for someone in need.

They say that actions speak louder than words. Does your action towards your neighbors indicate to that person that you love God? In other words, do you reflect God? Do your actions and attitude towards your neighbors show how much you really love God? Do you even love the people around you? How do you treat them? Would God be pleased? These are questions you need to ask yourself and get a completely truthful answer. I can tell you now, if you cannot stand the person sitting next to you at church, at work, on the bus, then the love of God does not flow through you. You are only fooling yourself saying that you love God, because you really do not. If you cannot love the people that God loves, then He's not in you because He loves His people through you. You're probably asking, "Well, what does God look like in a person?" you will see God in a person,

1. By the way they speak to you.
2. By the way in which they treat you.
3. By their love towards individuals.
4. By them helping those who are in need.
5. By their compassion towards others.

Their overall attitude to someone they do not know, is it nice, or were they mean? Yes, you can have a bad day, but that should not reflect the way you treat an individual. Well, is the person mean everyday or are they nice every day?

In John 13:23 they were leaning on Jesus' breast when He announced that His soul was troubled because He was going to die the next day. I like this story because although Jesus was heavy in spirit and troubled, He could have easily rejected them by telling them to get off, not now. But in-spite of how He felt, He did not reject the leaning, or speak harshly, or even push the person away, and this is the example we have to live by. Yes, we are all growing and are works in progress; but there's a standard, and Jesus painted the picture.

You know sometimes when we go through a depressing time we do not even want our children, our spouse, or our loved ones to touch us. We just want to be left alone. We make it known that we do not want to be touched or bothered. Jesus did not stop John from leaning on Him and He was hurting so badly that He had to mention it. He could not keep the hurt in any longer to Himself and had to express it, yet He allowed John to lean on Him. He did not tell John to move, I do not feel like it today or no such like manner, but yet we do it. Now, we all cannot be like Jesus overnight; but the whole goal and purpose on earth is to be like Him. It is not and will not be easy, but God is the One who transforms us and not we in and of ourselves. So if you're not there yet to where you love God enough to treat your neighbors right, don't beat yourself up over it. God will help you to get there; He will get you to love Him like that. He will wait for you; He will wait until you do.

There was a time that I did not love God as I do now; and let me tell you, it is a love that even I cannot explain. I love Him so much that I don't know what to do with myself sometimes because of how much I want Him, and how much I want to be with Him. I am so gone over Him that no matter what, I have to be with Him. I have to please Him. I was born for this reason. If I die right now, I would be happy because I will see Him and I will be with Him. As Paul puts it, "To be with Him is far better but to be here is more profitable for you." It takes time not only to build a relationship with God but to also build a history with Him.

BUILDING A HISTORY WITH GOD

Building a history with God, by this I mean things that you will go through in life and are even now going through as you read this book. We all go through things and will always go through until we leave this world. It is up to us how we handle things as they come.

Psalms 34: 19 states: *Many evils confront the [consistently] righteous, but the Lord delivers him out of them all.*

When you go through, you see that God had brought you out of that situation. A situation that you thought might have killed you has now made you stronger and you see that God has brought you out. I know that when we're going through some rough times we get afraid and wonder if God was ever going to bring us out, and we panic. The next time you go through something you will reflect on the last time you went through something and you will remember what God had done for you and you say, "If God brought me out of that, He will bring me out of this."

1. You see that God has brought you through a divorce.
2. You see that God has brought you through child abuse.
3. You see that God has brought you through sexual abuse
4. You see that God has brought you through physical and mental abuse.
5. You see that God has brought you through drug and alcohol addiction.

God brought you through all the things that you had to endure in life. Yes, it was very difficult at that time and you thought that you could have never made it, but look at you now. You are alive. The gift of life is precious and you're also clothed and in your right mind. Thank God the devil did not wipe you out. Some people who had gone through the same things that you have gone through are dead or in a mental institution but you're still here, alive and kicking and in your right mind.

Matthew 24:13 Jesus states: *But he who endures to the end will be saved.*

You see all the things that God has done for you and how God has been merciful to you by doing all these things for you.

1. He brought you out of prison.
2. He brought you out of your sicknesses.
3. He brought you out of a homosexual relationship.
4. He bought you out of that person's bed and you did not get AIDS or an STD.
5. He brought you out of your homeless situation.
6. He brought you out of your deathbed.

You've seen all the various things that God has brought you out of and your mind is still intact. You see that you are in your right mind and that He has brought you out many a time, and that's getting and building history with God. It's you seeing and getting flashbacks when you're in another situation you'll say, if God has done this for me once He will do it for me again. When you see those things happen in your life and how God has brought you out every time, you will love Him a little more than the time before. God's love is strong enough and will last until you come around. He's not like us who bail out because things aren't going our way; He can and will wait it out. He loves you that much.

WHAT'S THE PRICE FOR YOUR SOUL?

THE DIFFERENT KINDS OF LOVE

In the Greek there are four different names for love. There is Eros, Phileo, Sterge, and Agape. When we say, "I love you" one of these is what we're talking about. We are the only ones that use the word "love" for a variety of things, which have different meanings and levels of what we are saying or trying to say.

EROS

Eros is a love that gratifies the flesh, which simply indulges and satisfies the desires of the flesh. It also looks for reciprocity meaning what I do for you I expect you to also do for me and vice versa.

1. It is a love that has sexual desires.
2. It is a love that is of a personal nature.
3. It is a love that has much excitement.
4. It is also a love that can turn into hate.

It is the only kind of love that can turn on you just as quickly and as easily. It is not the kind of love with which God loves His church. It is a kind of love where we see an individual and fall passionately in love and a few years (if that long), it dies. It is more an infatuation than love.

2 Samuel 13, it talks about a brother and a sister who were of different mothers but the same father. He loved his sister and wanted to be with her but did not know how to do it. Then he got an idea from one of his cousins about what to do, and he took the advice and ran with it. The advice was to pretend to be sick and have his sister cook and feed him when he was left alone with her and then force her to have sex with him. After the sex act he no longer wanted her and he chased her. If he had asked his father

for her he would have given her to him; but because he forced her, he no longer wanted her.

Verse 15 states: *Then Amnon hated her exceedingly, so that his hatred for her was greater than the love in which he had loved her. And Amnon said to her, get up and get out.*

Amnon was more infatuated with his sister more so than he was in love with her.

INFATUATION

Infatuation is a feeling that feels just like love and is very intense. It is a feeling that you are aware of how much you want the person and would do anything for the individual for a while. It fools you into thinking that you are in love but in reality, you're in lust. Once you get the individual in bed, you will then lose your feelings (not always immediately) and you will not want to do anything for that person or even want to be with that person anymore as much as you once did. You've heard the saying, "It's a thin line between love and hate;" well, so is infatuation. It is a kind of love that can hate you as much as it once thought it loved you. It is a kind of feeling that is so intense that it also ends up with you beating each other's brains out in the parking lot. There is no genuine love for each other, and eventually your feelings of love wear away. You no longer want to be with that person.

1. You do not want to do anything for the person.
2. You do not want to touch that person.
3. They irritate you quickly and easily.
4. You argue just to leave the house.
5. You want to be with someone else.
6. You don't come home sometimes.
7. You end up hitting the person.

8. You end up hating the person.
9. You end up divorced.

From the time you feel hatred and dissatisfaction towards your spouse, you are in a state of un-fulfillment. As much as you try to make it work, it just cannot because the love is gone which was never really there in the first place. You became settled and got a comfort, not a good comfort but a sense of contentment that you know you have to go to work and not see the person all day long. You get busier and busier not because you want to work but just because you do not want to be there. You do not want them to even give a hint that they want to make love. That thought would turn your stomach.

As a Christian, you try harder to make things work, even going as far as staying with someone who abuses you. According to some, it's forbidden to get a divorce. You should have no such thought of divorce, so you try harder and harder and you become guilty because you feel the way you do. God knows and understands that that was not the person for you in the first place. He allows you not to be in a situation that will cause you anymore discontentment and discomfort than you've already been in. He releases you from that situation and now it's up to you to forgive yourself and move on. Although the other person may still want you, you still have to let that go. It is now a part of your past. Do not use your children as an excuse for why you're still trying to be friends with your ex. If your children are grown, then it simply means that you still feel guilty. If so, then you need to remarry that person and remove your guilt. If you do not wish to remarry that person then leave them alone and move on with your life so that the other can also move on with theirs' and not have any false hope that you two may get back together.

PHILEO

Phileo is a love of food and of animals even the affection of a friend and the love of the brethren, which are also the Christians. It is the love for other people that we do not know. When we tell anyone that we love them other than our family and husbands and wives, this is the love we're talking about.

1. We say we love our friends.
2. We say we love our neighbor.
3. We say we even love someone we see on TV.
4. We say we love our pastors.
5. We say we love our dog.
6. We say we love pizza.

This is the love we're talking about when we say we love these things. It is the one we use most often, sometimes even to our spouse. We end up just liking them as friends instead of Eros or Agape and we try to make a marriage work on this kind of love. That would never last. A marriage would not last if you have only phileo for the individual; you are more roommates and friends than lovers. You end up having relations with other people other than the one in your own house and in your own bed. Phileo is what we have for those that we consider friends and not lovers. It may start out as phileo but can end up as Eros. You may make a marriage but you may forget to add the agape. That is how and why people end up divorced.

STERGE

Sterge is the love of the family whoever they may be. We consider our family to be closer than that of any other. We try to protect them more so than we would any other. It is the kind of love where we could and / or would die for these people if necessary.

1. We love our children.
2. We love our aunts, uncles and cousins.
3. We love our brothers and sisters.
4. We love our parents.
5. We love our spouses.

When we're telling our family that we love them, this is what we are talking about. It is more meaningful than the rest because we would do more for our family than we would do for others, at least that is what most people would think and say.

AGAPE

Agape is the one that people seem to have most problems with, which is pure and genuine love. It is a diverse kind of love. This is the one that God has for the church. It is the one He said that husbands must have for their wives. The diversity is for your neighbors, your friends, money, your loved ones, and even your love for places. This is the kind of love Jesus talks about that you should have one for another.

1 Corinthians 13:4-8 states:

> *Love endures long and is patient and kind: love is never envious nor boils over with jealousy, is not boastful or vainglorious, does not display itself haughtily. It is not conceited (arrogant and inflated with pride); it is not rude (unmannerly) and does not act unbecomingly. Love (God's love in us) does not insist on its own rights or its own way, for it is not self-seeking; it is not touchy or fretful or resentful; it takes no account of the evil done to it [it pays no attention to a suffered wrong]. It does not rejoice at injustice and unrighteousness, but rejoices when right and truth prevail. Love bears up under anything and everything that comes, is ever ready to believe the best of*

every person, it hopes are fadeless under all circumstances, and
it endures everything [without weakening]. Love never fails
[never fades out or becomes obsolete or comes to an end].

This kind of love will always be there.

1. Love is something that you will always do.
2. Love is who God is.
3. Love is always looking to lend a helping hand.
4. Love is always seeking the lost.
5. Love is always giving to those that are less fortunate.
6. Love will always keep on loving to the end.

It is not easy to carry out this kind of love, but the God in you is love and He will help you to love even when it's hard to do.

Love is very hard to put into just one word. It is also not to be played with. A heart that's broken is a heart that hates, that's a covering of protection that is hard to penetrate or break through. When the right one comes along you end up treating them like the one that hurt you and you lose out in the end. You become callus and go about life not only with a don't-care attitude but you also have unforgiveness in your heart. God did not intend for you to wallow in the mud for years. He had every intention of bringing you out if only you had turned to Him.

God loves us so much that it hurts Him when we hurt. The kind of love God has for us is an everlasting love. He wants to give us that kind of love one for another. He wants to love us through our spouses; but if we do not give Him our lives He will not be able to give love through us to those that we want to call our own. Love is a very special thing that should not to be taken for granted; it's to be appreciated. Love can last a lifetime if it's with the right person and with you giving God your life so that He can teach you and show you what true love can be and what it's all about.

CHAPTER 13
FEELING FRUSTRATED

So you've been a Christian for years and you feel frustrated because you still do not have what God promised you and you may have given up. You may have thrown in the towel, putting your hands up saying, "That's it. I've had enough." What did Paul say in times like these?

Galatians 6:9 states:

And let us not lose heart and grow weary and faint in acting noble and doing right, for in due time and at the appointed season we shall reap, if we do not loosen and relax our courage and faint.

Paul is saying not to faint because we will reap in due time. With God sometimes (more often than not), things take longer than expected or even anticipated, but those who endure to the end shall reap their rewards. Don't be so quick to give up; ask God to help you with patience and He will. To me, patience was one of the hardest things I had to go through. It took years to be as patient as I am today; it was not easy. God had told me who my husband was but He never released us to each other. God was still preparing us for each other. I expected a lot from a man, and if he had come the wrong way to me it would have turned me off. I would have walked away because that was my forte. I would walk away just as easily and forget about a man that God said was mine. It would have left a bad taste in my mouth; and no matter what you do, if I make up my mind to let you go there's no way you will ever come back into my life, no matter how good you are. You see, God knows what's best and it was so rough that I had even told God I did not want this anymore because it was taking too long, and I felt that he was old enough to overcome all his problems and situations by now; but it was also me. So God was working on me as well.

GOD KNOWS WHEN

God knows when to bring about your blessing and at just the right time. God also wants to see what you will do if it does not happen. Would you still love Him? Will you still praise Him? Would you just give up on Him and go back to your old ways? Well, many of us had given up and turned to our old ways not willing to go through the process. You may want an anointing like someone else you admire, but are you willing to pay the price they paid? As someone once said, "If you could get the same anointing without giving up anything, then why do I have to give up things?" You cannot want another's anointing and do not want to go through the hardship they did. It was through that hardship that they gave birth to a relationship with God and to their ministry. Great power comes with and from great hardship and suffering. If you're not willing to or want to go through, you will never achieve. We all want something for nothing; it just does not work that way. There's a price to be paid. You've heard the saying, "Nothing in life is free." Even salvation was not free; God gave His life for you to be free. What are you willing to give up? What are you willing to do for it? How long are you willing to wait for it? How much are you willing to pay for it? It cost Him something; actually, it cost Him everything. Martin Luther King Jr. paid a price for us to be free. It cost him his life. Many men and women (whether it's in the bible or even today) of God (such as Job, Elijah, David) and many others had to go without and were at the verge of giving up, including me.

1. With people talking and laughing at them.
2. With people wanting to kill them.
3. With them being stricken with illnesses.

4. With them being without a place to live.
5. With them being without money.
6. With them being without food to eat.

And a whole lot more. So, why because you're going through something to help you grow and to better your life, you're willing to jump out of the fire? Don't you know that if you jump from the fire you will eventually have to go back in again? So don't come out before you're cooked. Make sure you're fully done, and God will take you out all on His own.

Isaiah 48:10 states: *Behold I have refined you, but not as silver; I have tried and chosen you in the furnace of affliction.*

God is building Christ-like character in you. It does not feel good. I know it, but you'll be better in the long run. You'll end up thanking God for unanswered prayers because God knows better what you need than you do. I have thanked God many times for prayers that He did not answer. Things I was praying for were not God's best, but I could not see it at that time; I sure see it now. What I thought I wanted was definitely not what I needed. It would have been a bigger disaster if I had gotten it. I would have been very unhappy and miserable, and I would have ended up blaming God for allowing me to have it.

When you're going through, it does not seem like God cares so you keep on asking, "God, where are You?" You get no answer, but just keep on praying; keep on holding on because only those that endure get the prize. I have been laughed at, mocked, and even been ridiculed for standing and trusting God when I could not even trace Him. But after all that, this was what He said, "My daughter, you've been faithful. You stood when it was hard to stand and I'm proud of you." When He told me that I cried because God said He was proud of me and I did nothing that He would be because of my behavior sometimes, but this encourages me to keep on going; and He's saying the same thing about you. There's a song that I love that says,

> The road gets rough and the going gets tough and the hills are hard to climb; I started out a long time ago there is no doubt in my mind, but I've decided to make Jesus my choice

And another one

> He never promise that the cross would not be heavy and the mountains too hard to climb but He promised that help would always come in time.

Not your time, but God's time. So be faithful in what you are doing. If you have given up, ask God to forgive you and pick it up again. If God has promised you something, it will come to pass. Do not think of something yourself and say that God promised you; God will not do what you thought He said, He will only do what He actually said.

Habakkuk 2:3 states:

> *For the vision is yet for an appointed time and it hastens to the end [fulfillment]; it will not deceive or disappoint. Though it tarry, wait [earnestly] for it, because it will surely come; it will not be behindhand on its appointed day.*

The first tarry simply means that it will take a while; the second tarry means that when it does come it shall come and waste no time coming. It will come quickly when you least expect. So you have to wait for it; don't be in such a hurry. God is transforming you to receive what He has for you. We are always in a hurry to get the blessing (me too), but it will come at the right time. Just when you think you cannot take it anymore, there it is.

THE TEA CUP

I heard a story of a teacup that was so beautiful; it was on display and people from all over came to look upon and to admire it. When the people were gathered together the teacup told them its story.

I was not always this beautiful, it said. I used to be a lump of clay. I was minding my own business it went on to say, when a man came and picked me up. I was confused and afraid; I told him to put me down and how much I did not want to be bothered, to please leave me alone. As much as I screamed and shouted, he would not leave me alone and he did not put me down. No matter how much I turned and twirled, twisted and bent, I could not be free or come out of his hand. Then all of a sudden, he started messaging me and now I was screaming even more. He was hurting me and yet, he did not seem to care. I cried and I cried; and when I thought I couldn't take any more, he stopped.

I was so happy and felt so good that he had finally left me alone; however, as soon as I thought to relax a while, he started cutting parts of me off. I cried out saying, hey, I need that, how do you expect me to survive without it? I was hurting so badly that I felt weak and weary from all the screaming and the pain that I was feeling. When I thought I could take no more the cutting was over and I felt even better and relaxed myself. As soon as I had relaxed myself I felt such a heat that I thought I would fain, and the man shut the door. I was screaming to the top of my lungs, banging on the door for the man to let me out, but he just ignored my cry for help. When I was about to faint, the door opened and I was out. I was so happy that I was out and went to relax again but as soon as I relaxed myself, I was placed in the hottest fire imaginable. This was hotter and harder than all the rest of things that I went through so far. I was dying and could hardly scream anymore. When I was about to die, the man pulled me out again.

I sighed a breath of relief and said I had made it. When I thought it was over, the man started brushing me. I felt uncomfortable and uneasy, but nothing like I had gone through before. When it was all over, I saw myself in a mirror. I could not believe my eyes. I never thought it was me. I never knew I had such beauty inside; but my master knew me. I used to be a lump of clay, but now I'm on display.

This teacup was just like many of us whom God (our potter) has made us out of clay and made us into a beauty that He can put us out there when the time is right after we have suffered a while. It's not easy going through the fire but we are being refined. We are being made into what God wants us to be so we can do what it is that He has called us to do. He also took away wanting things more than Him and us being materialistic.

BEING MATERIALISTIC

So you build a history with God and your relationship with Him gets stronger. You always have to first build that foundation or the relationship will not last. It's always first about the material things, such as, houses, cars, lands, boats, money and all the other such likes, but when you build that relationship with God it's no longer about material things, but spiritual things. If it's still about material things then you do not yet have that relationship with Him.

I first came to God because I wanted to know if all the things the prophet was saying about me were true. God knows how to draw you to Himself. He knows what you like and yes, your greed and uses that against you to win you over to Him. Yes, I had greed, greed for power. I had worked hard and acquired things on my own without a man. I had a 5-bedroom, 2-story home with a pool, 5 houses down from Jacky Gleason. My children had their own rooms. I had an office—the works. Yet, I wanted more. You know the saying, "The more you get; the more you want." So He lured me by my greed for more power. I like to lead; I was a born leader.

As a little girl, if my friends did no do what I wanted, I would beat them up until they did. As an adult, it was my way or the highway. If you wanted to be my friend you had to do the work, as in, you have to do the calling. You have to come to my house. You have to pay for everything. You have to initiate where you wanted us to go and I either accept or decline. I thought I was all that and a bag of chips. I was a very selfish person and a bad friend. I could not stand someone being late, but I could be as late as I wanted to be and my friends (if they wanted to continue being my friends) could not say a word.

I was a Personnel manager in charged of over three hundred people. I hired, fired, did orientation, trained, did the payroll, taught them how to invest and a few other things. I was not saved at the time and I was twenty-five years old when I got the position. Before I was a personnel manager, I was a store manager still doing the hiring, firing and payroll as well as ordering items that the store needed, and before that I was a nurse working in the hospitals, nursing homes, hospice, and of course private duty which paid much more than all the rest. I was very young when I became a nurse, and I really did not like it because my goal was to one day be in charge of a hospital, so when I got the manager's position I was pleased because I now worked in a position that I loved. So of course, my craving for power and for being in charged finally came to reality. I was doing all my duties as I should; but I was in a position to either hire you or not, fire you or give you another chance and any other things I could do to mess people's lives up or to help them. Although I was in that position, I did not abuse it too much because as mean as I was on the outside and as mean as I tried to pretend to be, I was not really that mean on the inside. I could not do anything to hurt them purposefully. I was able to do other things like tell them I did not have time to see them because I became mother to grown folks. When they needed to talk, from their personal private lives to their work and everything in between, they would have to make an appointment and if I determined (because I had discernment at that age), that they needed advice right away I would see them that same day. I had it in my power to do anything to them as I wished but I helped them more than I hindered them because God was working on me at that time knowing that one day I will be in even a greater and higher position. I had to always lead. I had to be in charge. So I had to check out this thing to see if it was real.

GOD'S AGENDA

I came to God with an agenda, but He knew my agenda and changed it to His agenda. I no longer have that greed for power, yet He has placed me in a position of power. Why? He took out the ugly from me and left me with the nice and good. The good is good, but you see we all come with different agendas. You know you have one or at least had one.

You might have come to God with the intensions that you were going to get a lot of money, or a big house, or fancy cars, and when it did not happen you were ready to quit. What you don't understand, is that God has His own agenda for your life. His agenda is to make you like His precious Son Jesus. His agenda is transforming you and giving you Christ-like character. It hurts becoming like Christ. It's like trimming a tree so that the tree can grow better and produce more fruit. It's the same way with us, except we feel our branches coming off and we think we need that branch to survive; but if God is taking it away it's because we definitely do not need it, and because it's a hindrance. God has to trim us; sometimes a big part of your tree has got to go, and you're there crying for what you've lost instead of rejoicing for what's to come.

Luke 13:6-9 states:

And He told them this parable: a certain man had a fig tree, planted in his vineyard, and he came looking for fruit on it, but did not find [any]. So he said to the vinedresser, see here! For these three years I have come looking for fruit on this fig tree and I find none. Cut it down! Why should it continue also to use up the ground [to deplete the soil, intercept the sun, and take up room]? But he replied to him, leave it alone, sir, [just] this one more year, till I dig around it and put manure [on the soil]. Then perhaps it will bear fruit after this; but if not, you can cut it down and out.

God is awesome and He wants us to succeed not only in life but also in what He has planned and willed for us, and He will do whatever it takes to ensure this. God gives us another chance. He wants us to bear fruit. He wants us to be a blessing to others, and He will help us to become what He wants us to be. I know that when you are going through, it's hard to see anything else. It's hard to see that any good could come from it.

I Romans 8:28 states: *We are assured and know that [God being a partner in their labor] all things work together and are [fitting into a plan] for good to and for those who love God and are called according to [His] design and purpose.*

God will always do things for your good and it will work out not just for you and whom you can help, but also for God's glory.

1. God makes what the enemy meant for evil to work out for your good.

2. God uses the enemy to get you to where He wants you to be.
3. It all fits right into God's plan for your life.
4. It will end up being a blessing in your life.

I have been there; it looks hopeless. Like all hope is gone and you're wondering what you have done to deserve this. And why do I have to go through this? And why do I have to hurt so much? All you're doing is making things worse by complaining, and you will have to go another lap around that same mountain. Instead of asking, "Why me?" Just thank the Lord that whatever it is that He is allowing you to go through right now, that it is for your benefit. It is for your wellbeing, just say,

> Although I do not understand it, I give You praise anyway; the Psalms says to praise You in all things and since You know what's best for me; I thank You because it's for Your glory. I thank You for bringing me out of this situation and whatever it is that You want me to learn from this, please let me know it.

You will be surprised how fast you will overcome your struggles. It's all in your attitude, and it's all in your praise how long your trouble will last. It's all up to you whether or not you stay in or you come out of your situation. I've been there, I know. Don't let your impatience keep you back or out of your promised land. Remember, you will reap if you faint not.

CHAPTER 14
IS YOUR LIFE AT A STAND STILL?

Is your life at a standstill? Why? How do you recognize that your life is at a standstill? Are you doing what God commanded you? Is your life pleasing to Him? Or is He disappointed in you? Are you growing spiritually? How do you know that you are? These are questions believers should ask themselves. In the next two chapters you will have the answer to these questions, and it will help your growth in Christ. Remember to be opened-minded and not closed-minded. If you are closed-minded, you will not learn; and if you don't learn you cannot grow.

There are three things you must identify:

1. How long have you been a Christian?
2. How much or how little have you grown?
3. In what way have you grown?

Make sure you do not use any excuses for why you are the way you are. We're trying to make your life better. Only those who are true to themselves will be able to change for the better. No excuses on why you have not changed or do not blame your past such as all the negative things that you've been through since childhood. I know these things are bad that have happened to you. These things, helped to shape you, but they do not determine who you are, or what you can become, or what God wants you to be. The enemy put those things in your path to destroy you, but you're still standing. You're still here. That's because you're stronger than you think and God had His hands on you. Look how far you've come. So we will put aside all the bad things that have happened in your life and move on with the real you. Let's get on with the person that you really are inside that is being hidden, and camouflaged with anger, hatred, and unforgiveness.

Hebrews 12:1-2 states:

Therefore then, since we are surrounded by so great a cloud of witnesses [who have borne testimony to the truth], let us strip off and throw aside every encumbrance (unnecessary weight) and that sin which so readily (deftly and cleverly) clings to and entangles us, and let us run with patient endurance and steady and active persistence the appointed course of the race that is set before us. Looking away [from all that will distract] to Jesus, who is the leader and the source of our faith [giving the first incentive for our belief] and is also its Finisher [bringing it to a maturity and perfection]. He, for the joy [of obtaining the prize] that was set before Him, endured the cross, despising and ignoring the shame, and is now seated at the right hand of the throne of God.

You have to put aside everything that has hurt you in the past and focus now on Jesus who is the only One that can truly bring you out and not let what happened in your past affect your future. We will break through these barriers and get you a breakthrough, not a breakdown. Yes, it's hard to forget about the past but you have to move on with your future. The devil wanted to break your spirit ever since you were a child. Don't let him win. Whatever the situation might have been, you still survived it. There's a reason you survived. Many people have been through similar situations and they're not living today, but you are. You had gotten the strength by the help of God to survive it, so let's not have a pity party but a praise party instead. Praise God that He brought you out of that mess. Now renew your mind.

RENEWING YOUR MIND

You might ask, well, how do I get on with my life after what I've been through, and how do I renew my mind, and what does all this mean? We must first go to the scriptures. What did God say about getting on with your life?

Romans 12:1-2 states:

> *I appeal to you therefore, brethren, and beg of you in view of [all] the mercies of God, to make a decisive dedication of your bodies [presenting all your members and faculties] as a living sacrifice, holy (devoted, consecrated) and well pleasing to God, which is your reasonable (rational, intelligent) service and spiritual worship. Do not be conformed to this world (this age), [fashioned after and adapted to its external, superficial customs], but be transformed (changed) by the [entire] renewal of your mind [by its new ideals and its new attitude], so that you may prove [for yourselves] what is the good and acceptable and perfect will of God, even the thing which is good and acceptable and perfect [in His sight for you].*

You see, you first have to change your way of thinking by wanting within your own self to want to change. You have to tell yourself, there is more to me than what I've become.

And Philippians 3:13-15 states:

> *I do not consider, brethren, that I have captured and made it my own [yet]; but one thing I do [it is my one aspiration]: forgetting what lies behind and straining forward to what lies ahead. I press on toward the goal to win the [supreme and heavenly] prize to which God in Christ Jesus is calling us upward. So let those of us who are spiritually mature, full-grown have this mind and hold these convictions; and if in any respect you have a different attitude of mind, God will make that clear to you also.*

Whatever you want just do not fall into your lap, you have to do something and then your way will be prosperous. You have to reach for what you want and make a move and make something good happen in your life.

I know of a man who is very smart and has many good ideas and talents but does nothing about it because he feels that he would be automatically defeated. He thinks that his ideas would not work because there is so much competition out there; and because of all the negative things that have happened to him in the past, he would not even try. The devil has already defeated him because of his mindset and his fear of failing. He does not come out of the box but is stuffed inside and has outgrown it; and he cannot see all his potentials. He will always have a mediocre life and a mediocre mentality. He would end up living that less-than kind of life. With all his talents, he will end up wondering, "What if?" Do not be like that; if you have an idea, do not let the fear of failing or the fear of not making it deter you from trying. Those people who became great did not get it on the first, second or even the third try, but they did not give up and neither should you. Work your project until it works for you.

The years are quickly slipping away and you're not getting any younger. So make a decision that will have a meaningful impact on your life. It's time to make that change that you've been meaning to do, but did not know how or where to start. So you start here with being true to yourself and watch God change your life for the better. You have to learn how to let people go. It is something you have to do for yourself.

FORGIVENESS

So is also forgiveness. It is not for the other person. It is for you. You might ask, well, what do you mean forgiveness is for me and not the other person? Why should I forgive when they were the ones that have done me wrong? Well, you were the one that the wrong was done to.

1. You are the one who really has a difficult time not doing what you should do, causing pain upon your own self and making your life miserable.
2. You are the one that dislikes the person that's done the wrong holding in hate and bitterness.
3. You are the one that is holding back your life from progressing.

The people that have hurt you could come in different shape and form. In most cases, you knew the individual and you trusted them not to hurt you. You might have done things differently if you could have helped yourself especially if you were a child when the bad thing happened to you. You may have sat and cried many nights over what happened and how could they have done it, and why did you not do something about it?

1. It may be a man or a woman.
2. It may be someone you know or don't know.
3. It may be a pastor, an aunt or uncle.
4. It could even have been your mom or dad.

You cannot beat yourself up over what was done and you have to not cry over those things anymore. If you want to cry, you may cry now but let this be your farewell cry and then move on with your life. You've come a long way, so don't let the enemy draw you back into that feeling of loneliness.

No matter who it was that has done the wrong deed towards you; deep down inside you have developed hatred towards them. Wherever there's hatred, there is also bitterness and anger. You might have even said, "I will never forgive them for what they did to me." You might have even seen the person or persons and they are living their lives as happy as they could be, not even thinking about you; and here you are, still bitter over what they did. It's messing up your life; you're not moving on but at a place where you don't want to be but because you have such hate in you that you've put your life on hold and cannot move on.

When I was in the 12th grade I was engaged to a man that was the love of my life. He was two years ahead of me and in college. We had big plans where I was going to move from Florida to Canada after we got married because his student visa was up. It was not just he proposing (asking me to marry him) we had an engagement party where my pastor, friends and both our families were there. It was done exactly like a wedding. We exchanged vows except I only received an engagement ring. Well, six months before we got married we were fooling around and he asked me if it was okay for us to make love. Since I was a virgin and we were going to get married so soon, I said it was okay. It did not even seem like it was me when I said yes because I was a Christian and I knew better, but I could not help myself. I never thought anything would ever come between us since we were so inseparable. Nonetheless, I got pregnant. My very first and only time with him I got pregnant. I was very happy because the baby was formed out of love. When I told him, he was extremely happy and came down from Canada for us to get married right away.

When he came, I did not know his parents were trying to talk him out of being with me. He obviously was not listening to them and came and got me for us to go to the courthouse to get married. If I knew that his parents were trying to stop him from being with me I would not have said what I said. I wanted him so much and I did not understand myself why I even said what I said because that definitely was not me. When we got to the courthouse I stopped him and said, "I do not want to get married this way; I want our parents to be there." Like all girls, I wanted a decent wedding. We left the courthouse and went home. He had to leave the next day to go back to Canada. He came to see me before he left and everything seemed fine, but when he got back he called me the next day and told me that the child I was carrying was not his and how could I do this to him. I, of course, thought he was joking but he kept asking why did I do it? Why did I cheat on him? I was devastated, and no matter what I say I could not get through to him. I had to raise my child on my own. I did not want to finish high school; I stayed home wallowing in my pity, and what was a joyous thing became a shameful thing. I thank God that no matter how bad I was feeling I never contemplated suicide or abortion. Those things never ever entered my mind, but one thing entered, and that was to pray; and my prayer came true. My son's dad has no more children but the one that I have for him. I went back to school; and I thank God that I used to go to summer school because I was bored during summertime. I took driver's education just to past the time and because of that I had enough credits to graduate on time and with my class. (God is awesome).

I had now developed a hatred for men, and they all had to pay for what one man did to me. I was mean, spiteful and loved revenge; and no matter how mean and nasty I treated them they still came back for more. They often told me that I treated men like men treated women. All that is ladies; it's because men see the need and dependency that you have for them and they take advantage of it; but if you were your own woman and not depend on them then they will have no hold over you. They also test you to see what you will put up with and how far they can go; and whatever you permit they will push even further. I also compared every man that came my way to this so-called love of my life; I made him into something that he was not. I made him better than he was, and of course no one matched up. I became the love them and leave them, and a callousness came over my heart that I could not, or even wanted to, love anyone. I never let my guard down, and I never let anyone get that close to me again. I had such hatred and unforgiveness in my heart that it clouded my judgment. God had allowed many good men in my life that took care of me and would not hurt me but it did not matter. I hurt them and I enjoyed doing it. My family thought that I was blessed and because I had the "good hair" that I got all the good men; but the truth was I did nothing that they would want to stay with me, and yet they clung to me like magnet. I would never do anything nice; and if they complained that I did not treat them right, I would show them the door. I didn't play.

Anyway, to make a long story short, the day after I got out of the hospital, he called and asked me to marry him and out of hatred I said, "I will never marry you" and I hung up the phone. I saw him thirteen years later and he was already married and I was still single. When I saw him for the first time I said, "This is what I cried over all these years?" I, of course, had to get revenge; and every day that he was there, he cried over how he lost me. He then asked me to forgive him and I thought I could never do something like that much less talk to him knowing what he did to me; but I got the courage to say I forgive you, and I felt free. I wasted many years crying over someone I would not have ever chosen in my adult life. I was angry at myself for letting all those years go to waste when I could have had a good life with my very last boyfriend. He loved me and was willing to wait three years for me after I had accepted Jesus, but I could not let him do that because God had promised me some things. However, that was how God has orchestrated my life. I grew more than I ever thought I could, had I not gone through what I did. I am now friends with my oldest son's dad and I feel no hatred or animosity towards him or his family; and I owe it all to God with the rule of forgiveness.

When you saw those persons that have hurt you and have moved on with their lives you probably said, "How can they go on with their lives knowing what they have done to me?" Well, in order for that which you have deep down inside to be released, you have to forgive the person; and when you have forgiven them, you in yourself will feel a release. But this release will never come if you first do not forgive. When you forgive:

1. It releases authority in your life.
2. It takes the heavy weight off your shoulders.
3. It will make you feel light and free.
4. You will be able to move on with your life.

Matthew 6:14-15 states:

For if you forgive people their trespasses [their reckless and willful sins, leaving them, letting them go, and giving up resentment], your heavenly Father will also forgive you. But if you do not forgive others their trespasses [their reckless and willful sins, leaving them, letting them go, and giving up resentment], neither will your Father forgive you your trespasses.

We have done many things in our lives for which we ask God to forgive us; and when you go to God with unforgiveness in your own heart, how do you expect God to forgive you? If God has forgiven you and let you go, then you should forgive others and let them go also. You know that you have unforgiveness in your heart: If seeing the person brings up those ugly memories of what they have done. If when their name comes up and you feel tightness in the pit of your stomach. If your blood still boils when you hear their voice and if you see them and your hatred for them rises.

So forgiving is for your benefit. All these things can and will stop your growth in God. There's a deep root that caused you to be the way you are; and you have to find out what is the cause of your behavior, your disposition, and your attitude. These things will cause you to stunt your own growth. You get bitter and bitter instead of better and better. You must first find what the problem is that is holding you back. Finding your root cause is the first step to overcoming your stagnancy. Once you've found the real cause of what's holding you back, you can then take it from there and move on. You can then begin working on those things that you have found to be the source that was keeping you bound. You then have to release whatever these things are and ask God to forgive the individual or individuals that did this to you.

When you see that you are doing the same things over and over and that you're becoming meaner and meaner, you have to wonder why you're so mean. You have to want to make a change. You have to think of what you really want out of life and go after it. You have to do something about it. You have to make the move. You cannot stay mean all your life; no one will want to be around you; no one will want to be your friend. You could not figure out why you are the way you are, so you've come to the conclusion that this is the way I am and I'm not going to change, and you still have no growth. You need to get rid of that mindset. It's of the enemy; he wants to keep you bound. You have to make up in your mind that you not only want to change but that you're going to change and that you want to live fully for God, that you want your life to be a representation of Christ. So you set your will (that is to make up in your mind to do something), make that decision and stick to it no matter how rough it gets.

DO WHAT GOD SAY

Are you doing what God commanded you to do? Not growing could also mean that you have not done the last thing that God told you to do. You may have heard what God said and,

1. You may have been afraid to do it.
2. You may have forgotten what He told you to do.
3. You did not want to, or it was too difficult for you.

Unless you do what He said, you will be circling that same mountain and wondering what went wrong or why things aren't happening. God will only let you move to your last level of obedience. He will never let you move on to something else unless you do the last thing He told you to do.

Luke 6:46-49 states:

Why do you call Me, Lord, Lord, and do not [practice] what I tell you? For everyone who comes to Me and listens to My words [in order to heed their teaching] and does them, I will show you what he is like. He is like a man building a house, who dug and went down deep and laid a foundation upon the rock; and when a flood arose, the torrent broke against that house and could not shake or move it, because it had been securely built or founded on a rock. But he who merely hears and does not practice doing my words is like a man who built a house on the ground without a foundation, against which the torrent burst, and immediately it collapsed and fell, and the breaking and ruin of that house was great.

God always has your best interest at heart and if you do what He tells you to do, things will always work out for you.

1. God may have told you to leave someone.
2. God may have told you to speak to someone.
3. God may have told you to forgive someone.
4. God may have told you to give away something you like.
5. God may have told you to move to another state.

It could be an array of things that God might have told you to do and if you do not do it, then how can you move forward. Obedience is the key that will propel you to the next level. It requires obedience. The problem we have is that we are not aware of all the blessings that come with obedience.

1 Samuel 15:22 states: *Samuel said, has the Lord as great a delight in burnt offerings and sacrifices as in obeying the voice of the Lord? Behold to obey is better than sacrifice, and to hearken than the fat of rams.*

You may think that God is telling you to do this to hurt you, or to embarrass you but God is in the blessing business; and yes, you do have to work for it and obeying what He says is how you get the blessings. I know that forgiving someone is very difficult. As a matter of fact, I told one of my friends that she had to forgive her father for all the negative things that were said and done to her as a child. She could not stand being in the same room with him much less speak to him.

Just recently she spoke to him in person and told him that she forgave him. She then told me that she almost did not do it and how very difficult it was to say what she wanted to say. The enemy tried to trick her into telling her a phone conversation would do just fine, but she got the courage to speak to him in person. It was the hardest thing she ever had to do; she then said that the release she had could not be explained. She felt light and free. Now she wanted to tell everyone that did her wrong that she forgives them. When stubbornness sets in, it's hard to get rid of it. Ask anyone who had to forgive someone for the horrific things that they did to them; they will tell you that it was not easy, but they also felt great release after they forgave the individuals.

God wants us to forgive. He knows that when you forgive, your life will change for the better. That is why He urges us to hurry up and forgive. The enemy will lie to you and trick you where you would not want to forgive, and he will keep you bound. God will give you grace to go to the individual or individuals and release them, and when you do you will also release yourself.

CHAPTER 15
PLEASING GOD

Is your life pleasing to God? Or is He disappointed in you? This is a question that must be answered. As Christians we all want to please God, but wanting to please Him and doing so are two different things. You should not only want to please God, you must strive to please Him. You should go out of your way to please Him. You may be asking yourself, well, how do I please God? There are many ways to please God? You please God,

1. By simply doing what He tells you to do (obedience).
2. By keeping His commandments.
3. By reading your bible and meditating every day.
4. By praying every day.
5. By helping others as often as you can.
   a. Reaching out to the poor.
   b. Volunteering where you can.
   c. Visiting the prisons.
   d. Visiting the sick and shut-in.
   e. Reaching out to children.
6. By fasting to kill those things, which are not pleasing to God that reside in you.
7. By being nice to everyone, even if they're not nice to you.

Seeking God through prayer is the key to helping you do what He says. Only by seeking Him you will get to know His likes and His dislikes. Seeking Him helps you in ways that you would not dream possible. God cares and is concerned with every area of your life. Yes, He will even tell you what to wear. I have heard some people say that God does not have the time to involve Himself in such small matters and that He has much more important things to do, but what is more important to God than you?

Proverbs 3:5-6 states:

Lean on, trust in, and be confident in the Lord with all your heart and mind and do not rely on your own insight or understanding. In all your ways know, recognize, and acknowledge Him, and He will direct and make straight and plain your paths.

You have to learn to depend on God; it's not easy when you have never depended on anyone before. I was like that. I never depended on anyone; and when God told me to leave my job, I had to depend on Him to get my bills paid. When He told me to move to California I had to depend on Him even more because I knew no one there. When you depend on God, He will bring the things to you that He knows you have need of. Things can and will get tough, but when they do,

1. Do not look at what you see.
2. Do not form your own opinion.
3. Do not do anything on your own.
4. Always acknowledge God.
    a. Always ask Him what you should do.
    b. Always ask Him where you should go.
    c. Always ask Him whom you should be with.
    d. Always ask Him how you should invest.
        • Your time and your money.
5. Make sure you wait for an answer before making a move.
6. Make sure you get a conformation on your first answer.

God does not live in time and if you ask Him what you should or should not wear takes no time at all away from God. What, He's so busy that He has no time for the smaller things? Well that's not true. God does care what you wear, He wants you always to look your best, be at your best. He caters for that.

Maybe God will not tell you what to wear everyday but I know and I guarantee that if you take the time out to ask Him, He will put it in your heart and in your mind what to wear. I know my Father and how He works and if He works like that with me, He will most certainly work like that for you. Why? Did not the bible say that He's no respecter of persons? Did He not say to acknowledge Him in all your ways? So why would He not be concerned over what you wear?

There was a dinner one year at my church [the city of refuge] where Bishop Noel Jones is the presiding pastor. I had no intentions of going to this dinner because at that time I really did not eat past 6p.m. God, however, wanted me to go and He even told me what to wear out of my closet. I had a few evening dresses and although I knew which one God told me to wear, I decided to try on a few to see how they fitted; but none fitted the way I liked. And when I finally tried on the one that God had said, it fitted exactly the way I wanted.

On another occasion, one day when I was going out I put an outfit on but I did not know that one side was thinner than the other; and the Holy Spirit said, "Change your top." When I looked in the mirror I saw that my bra was showing, so I had to take the shirt off.

That's just two examples of how God will tell you what to wear and what not to wear. If I did not go to that dinner it would have displeased my Father and I would have been in disobedience. It pleases God when you obey Him because it helps you in the long run. You may not understand why God asks you to do something. Instead of trying to figure out why, just trust that God knows best and do it anyway. Pleasing God comes from loving God. The bible tells us what God wants for us, what He expects of us, how we should behave, how to live our lives, how to please Him, and how to respond to Him. God will always be a part of our lives doing things for us that we did not ask for, but that we need.

Matthew 6:28-30 states:

> *And why should you be anxious about cloths? Consider the lilies of the field and learn thoroughly how they grow; they neither toil nor spin. Yet I tell you, even Solomon in all his magnificence (excellence, dignity, and grace) was not arrayed like one of these. But if God so clothes the grass of the field, which today is alive and green and tomorrow is tossed into the furnace, will He not much more surely cloth you, o you of little faith?*

God will always be looking after us even in the little things. You may be without today but God will give you back more than you ever had before. I know because I was there. He helps us and wants us growing spiritually.

SPIRITUAL GROWTH

Growing spiritually is a vital part of our Christian walk. God wants His children to grow. If you had a child and he or she was two years old and was not walking, you would be concerned. If the child were five years old and still was not talking you would be concerned. You would take the child to a physician and state the areas of concern. After examining the child the doctor comes back and tells you that the child had a defect or some kind of disease. They had to look for the root cause to why the child was not growing. Well, it's the same way when a Christian is not growing, there is something wrong; however, we do not think that anything is wrong with us and we go about our business like there's nothing wrong when deep inside you know that there is. Well, ignoring the problem is worse than confronting it. If you ignore the problem, don't think for one bit that it will go away, because it won't, it will just get worse. The difference here is that your life depends on this and it seems like you just don't care.

It's like people who are sick and they know that they are, but they would not go to the doctor because they're afraid that the doctor will give them something. What they are really afraid of is that their sickness would be terminal; and to them, not knowing is better than knowing. So they would rather not know and die than to know and do something about it and live. The doctor will not do anything to harm you or they would not put any sickness upon you. People would rather not know that they have something wrong, so they ignore it and what could have saved their lives, causes them to die. Well, your spiritual growth is that important and more because it determines where you will spend eternity. You have to identify the problem and what is the cause of you not growing spiritually.

1. Identify the root cause.
2. Know the reason why you're not growing spiritually.
3. Go to the spiritual doctor (Jesus) to help you to remove the problem.
4. Walk the walk that Jesus has placed in you to do.

Growing spiritually is the way for you to move on with God, which causes you to bear fruit.

BEARING FRUIT

We all need to bear fruit. The whole purpose of being saved is to bear fruit. You may be asking what is bearing fruit? Well bearing fruit is being able to speak to another person and cause them to make a change. How do you know that you are bearing fruit?

1. Bearing fruit is speaking to a person and them accepting Jesus as Lord and Savior of their lives.
2. Bearing fruit is being able to speak to someone who has done you wrong without animosity.
3. Bearing fruit is taking the hate out of your heart.
4. Bearing fruit is showing love to people who are not nice to you.

Jesus has set a standard and an example of how we should be and what we need to do to produce fruit.

John 15:1-2 states:

I am the true vine, and my father is the vinedresser. Any branch in me that does nor bear fruit [that stops bearing] He cuts away (trims off, takes away); and He cleanses and repeatedly prunes every branch that continues to bear fruit, to make it bear more and richer and more excellent fruit.

What is fruit and how do I bear it? Fruit is the evidence of your spiritual growth. The things you've learned by reading your bible, by listening to sermons, by going to bible study, and by praying everyday. Eventually, these things take root in your life and cause growth. When growth comes you, in turn, reach out to people and tell them about Jesus and what He's done for you. Now, this is fruit.

John 15:5-6 states:

I am the vine; you are the branches. Whoever lives in Me and I in him bears much (abundant) fruit. However, apart from Me [cut of from vital union with Me] you can do nothing. If a person does not dwell in Me, he is thrown out like a [broken-off] branch, and withers; such branches are gathered up and thrown into the fire, and they are burned.

When you bear fruit you will do things to show forth your growth. The things that are within you will come out to those around you.

1. You witness to a lost soul.
2. You encourage and lift up people's spirit.
   a. You tell them that they will be all right.
   b. You tell them that God will always be there.
   c. You tell them that you'll be praying for them.
3. You're always looking for those in need.
4. You will be faithful in all that you do.

You normally start with those around you. You always start out small with one or two persons a week and then it gradually go up from there. You then expand to your neighbors and then to the streets. By doing this you are showing fruit and you are now being productive. How do you know that you are growing spiritually?

1. You are growing spiritually when you see that you're not cursing out anyone like you used to do.
2. You are growing spiritually when you no longer go to the strip club or whatever it was that you use to go.
3. You are growing spiritually when you look at yourself and not recognize you; even your friends can see that you've changed.
4. You are growing spiritually when you are much nicer than you've ever been, by praying for those who were not nice to you and by paying your tithes and offering.

If you're not doing these things then you need to check yourself to see if you are learning anything from what you read, hear in sermons; or your prayer life may not be up to par. It may be that what you hear goes in one ear and out the other. If you're not doing these things then you are not doing as Jesus said you should do.

Luke 6:27-36 states:

But I say unto you who are listening now to Me: [in order to heed, make it a practice to] love your enemies, treat well (do good to, act nobly toward) those who detest you and pursue you with hatred, invoke blessings upon and pray for the happiness of those who curse you, implore God's blessing (favor) upon those who abuse you [who revile, reproach, disparage, and high-handedly misuse you]. To the one who strike you on the jaw or cheek, offer the other jaw or cheek also; and from him who takes away your outer garment, do not withhold your undergarment as well. Give away to everyone who begs of you [who is in want of necessities], and of him who takes away from you your goods, do not demand or require them back again. And as you would like and desire that men would do to you, do exactly so to them. If you [merely] love those who love you, what quality of credit and thanks is that to you? For even the [very] sinners love their lovers (those who loves them). And if you are kind and good and do favors to and benefit those who are kind and good and do favors to and benefit you, what quality of credit and thanks is that to you? For even the preeminently sinful do the same. And if you lend money at interest to those from whom you hope to receive, what quality of credit and thanks is that to you? Even notorious sinners lend money at interest to sinners, so as to recover as much again. But love your enemies and be kind and do good [doing favors so that someone derives benefit from them] and lend, expecting and hoping for nothing in return but considering nothing as lost and despairing of no one; and then your recompense (your reward) will be great (rich, strong, intense, and abundant), and you will be sons of the Most High, for he is kind and charitable and good to the ungrateful and the selfish and wicked.

God said that you must be different from those that are in the world (that is, those people who have not accepted Jesus into their lives). You must be different because Christ lives in you. To show forth that you have grown is what you do when these obstacles come your way.

1. If someone curses you.
2. If someone hits you.
3. If someone lies on you.
4. If someone tries to frame you.
5. If someone causes you to lose your money.
   i.   Whether they stole it outright.
   ii. Whether they made you to invest wrongfully.
   iii. Whether they borrowed from you and would not pay you back.

When you find yourself doing the right things if these obstacles come your way, then you have grown spiritually and have graduated to the next level in your Christian walk. It is not easy to do these things but as you draw closer to God you will find that it is natural and easy as well.

CHAPTER 16
WHY SHOULD YOU GIVE?

When you love God you will want to give. He said in His word that you should give to test and prove Him. This is the only time God said that you are allowed to test and prove Him; and He will welcome it. God will give you a seed and then ask it again of you knowing that you need it; and if you would willingly give it back to Him, He will automatically double, triple, quadruple it when He gives it back to you. If you do not give, God said that you are not just cursed but you are cursed with a curse. You will be robbing God (of what He has given to you in the first place) if you don't pay or give your tithes and offerings as He commanded. If and when you do pay your tithes and offerings, God said that He would bless you. When He does bless you, it is for the furthering of His kingdom not just for yourself. You are not just to give tithes and offerings; you must also give to the poor. You must also give to the widowed. God said that if you do, you will be lending to Him, and He said, that you should owe no man anything. So if we lend to God that means He owe us. God is true to His word because He watches over His words to perform them. He will give back to you like He promised, but you first have to give. Here are a few reasons that you should give.

1. If you love God, you will automatically want to give.
2. If and when you give, you will be blessed.
3. If you do give, you will be lending to God.
4. If you do not give, you will never have enough.
5. If you do not give, you will be constantly putting your money in a bag full of holes, and when you reach in for some you will find none.
6. If you do not give, you will be robbing God.

Malachi 3:8-11 states:

Will a man rob or defraud God? Yet you rob and defraud Me. But you say, in what way do we rob or defraud you? [You have withheld your] tithes and offerings. You are cursed with the curse, for you are robbing Me, even this whole nation. Bring all the tithes (the whole tenth of your income) into the store house, that there may be food in My house, and prove Me now by it, says the Lord of Hosts, if I will not open the windows of heaven for you and pour you out a blessing, that there shall not be room enough to receive it. And I will rebuke the devourer [insects and plagues] for your sakes and he shall not destroy the fruits of your ground, neither shall your vine drop its fruit before the time in the field, says the Lord of Host.

God has made some distinct and very clear promises of what He will do if you give Him what is His. Just imagine that God is the one that gave you that job so you can pay all your bills, and all He asks in return is ten percent (10%) of your earnings. Whatever else you want to give as an offering that's up to you, but you do need to give it.

When I first got saved it was dropped in my spirit to give eleven percent. The ten percent is my tithes and the one percent is my free will offering. I do that no matter how much money I have so that I might be consistent in what I do, whether I make a million dollars or ten dollars. I do not give based on how I feel. By that I mean, if the pastor was not there I would still give. If I was upset that day, I would not withhold my giving. I would give every time. After I have given my tithes and offerings, whenever I go to church I still give an offering out of the little that I do have left. Ten percent might seem much to you but I guarantee you that if you are faithful in your tithes and offering, God will do just as He said in due time. He will make ends meet and you will be better off. There is a process that God has set up and that is,

1. God will give a seed.
2. You have to sow the seed.
3. You have to wait for the seed to die.
4. You then see what you've planted sprout.
5. You then reap a harvest.

This is the law of sowing and reaping. It's called agriculture. You first have to have seed to sow, and then you will reap a harvest over time much more than what you've sown; and you can still even keep from what you've harvested and sow again to reap again. However, if you do not have anything to sow or withheld what you do have, you will not and cannot reap anything what you have not sown. This process is forever planted in our hearts.

Genesis 8:22 states: *While the earth remains, seedtime and harvest, cold and heat, summer and winter, day and night shall not cease.*

So God gives the seed and you must plant. That is the law of planting and reaping. You may not see money right away but you will see that He will take care of things such as your car, your food, and your clothes. All your essentials will be taken care of. God has taken such good care of me. One day I drove forty miles from home to church on the freeway on a flat tire going eighty miles an hour and did not even know that it was flat until I got to church and someone told me that my tire was flat. I could tell you many things that God has done for me because I pay my tithes and offerings.

Do not be stingy with what God has allowed you to have.

1. You have to give of what He's given to you.
2. You have to give over and in abundance.
3. You have to give out of the willingness of your heart.
4. You will receive exactly what you give out.

Luke 6:38 states:

Give, and [gifts] will be given to you; good measure, press down, shaken together, and running over, will they pour into [the pouch formed by] the bosom [of your robe and used as a bag]. For with the measure you deal out [with the measure you use when you confer benefits on others], it will be measured back to you.

What you give shall be given back to you. That's what God said, and if He said it then it has to be true. In what way are you giving?

1. How much are you giving?
2. How often are you giving?
3. How is your heart when you give?
4. What do you expect in return?
   a. Are you giving just to get back?
   b. Are you giving because God said so?
   c. Are you giving because you want to and is the right thing to do?
5. What do you do when you're waiting for a return?
6. Do you give only when you feel like it?

You cannot out give God. You cannot beat God in giving. God will always give you more than you dreamed possible. When I was moving to California, God gave me two thousand dollars to move with; and on top of that He told me to cut all ties with my ex-boyfriend. When we arrived in California, (my two sons and my mother and me), we stayed in many hotels because I was not sure exactly where God wanted us to be. All I knew was L.A. The money of course was running very low because it was not being replenished. We found a Chinese place that sold dollar rice and a dollar fifty meat. It was very good food. We also bought dollar burgers, dollar chicken sandwiches and we made do with what we had and were satisfied (thank God for the dollar menu). We may not have had what we were accustomed to, but God still provided. I trusted God. I know that He was going to make a way out, and after a while He did. Things did not happen right away. As a matter of fact, I wanted to go back to Florida because I thought I had made a mistake. I knew that I knew that I heard from God, but it was nothing like what He had said when we got there, and I thought that this was a huge mistake. It was not just me by myself, but I had others who were depending on me while I was depending on God. I never depended on anyone before and this was very difficult for me, but God wanted me to depend on Him and I had no choice because I knew no one, and the one that could have helped, God told me to cut all ties with him. I did not understand it before, but now I know that when I was going through I could have simply called my ex-boyfriend to get me out of my situation instead of staying in the fire until God brought me out. God will allow you to go thought some things to see if you will still love Him no matter what. If you stick it out, He will bless your socks off. God provided, we never went to bed hungry and we never needed anything that God did not provide.

Remember Abraham and Melchizedek when he gave him tithes of all, and God blessed him because of it? That was the first time that tithes were implemented. When you get what God has given you, there are certain things that you must do.

1. You must give God first.
2. You must give to others such as the poor and needy.
3. You must give to those who have nowhere to go.

Be willing to give back what God so graciously has given to you. You must seek out those who you can help to make their lives work and you will be blessed in return. One time I could not find my checkbook and I was not going to buy any groceries until I had taken my tithes and offering out before I started spending, it's that important to me. You cannot and never ever will out give God. Do not be afraid to give because you do not have enough, give what you have and God will bless you no matter what you gave.

Genesis 14:18-20 states:

> *Melchizedek king of Salem [later called Jerusalem] brought out bread and wine [for their nourishment]; he was the priest of God Most High. And he blessed him and said, blessed (favored with blessings, made blissful, joyful) be Abram by God Most High, possessor and maker of heaven and earth. And blessed, praised and glorified be God Most High, who has given your foes into your hand! And [Abram] gave him a tenth of all [he had taken].*

Abraham automatically gave to the Lord what God had allowed him to gain from the battle after he had gone to get Lot back. He wasted no time in giving what was freely given to him of God.

In Genesis 15:1 after Abraham had given all His tithes, God said: *After these things, the word of the Lord came to Abram in a vision, saying, Fear not, Abram, I am your Shield, your abundant compensation, and your reward shall be exceedingly great.*

God became Abraham's blessing and He gave him over and in abundance of what he expected.

Jacob, Abraham's grandson promised to give God a tenth of all God had given to Him.

Genesis 28:20-22 states:

> *Then Jacob made a vow, saying, if God will be with me and*
> *will keep me in this way that I go and will give me food to*
> *eat and clothing to wear, so that I may come again to my*
> *father's house in peace, then the Lord shall be my God and*
> *this stone which I have set up as a pillar (monument) shall be*
> *God's house [a sacred place to me], and of all [the increase of*
> *possessions] that You give me I will give the tenth to You.*

Jacob told God that if God would take care of him, he would give Him back a tenth of all God had granted unto him. That also should be our attitude of wanting to give back to God a tenth of everything He has given us. If you don't, then this is what will happen to you.

Haggai 1:6 states:

> *You have sown much, but you have reaped little; you eat, but*
> *you do not have enough; you drink, but you do not have your*
> *fill; you clothe yourselves, but no one is warm; and he who*
> *earns wages has earned them to put them in a bag with holes*
> *in it.*

This is what happens to those who do not pay their tithes. Have you ever wondered to yourself, "Where did all my money go?" You try to figure out what you spent it on and still came up with nothing. You thought you at least had some left over to put in the bank, only to find out that it's all gone. These are holes in your bag and you still cannot make ends meet.

Yes, sometimes when God is allowing you to go through your wilderness, God will not allow you to store up manna. He will give you what you need day by day. There are some of us who never want to give back to God and we spend and are never satisfied; and we cannot make ends meet because we say that we do not make enough to give.

When I first moved into my apartment, let's say that my rent was eight hundred dollars a month and I receive eight hundred dollars per month; I will automatically take out my eleven percent and obviously I was short, not only in my rent but also would have no money for the light bill, the phone bill and the other essentials; but I did not let that stop me from giving back to God what He has so graciously given to me. I did not say that I couldn't afford it because whatever I have belongs to God; and if I was short, once I pay my tithes and offering, it was then up to God to make ends meet. Remember, obedience is better than sacrifice. It was a little touch-and-go at times, but He always came through. A time or two I had to tell the landlady that I did not have the entire rent when it was due, but I ended up giving it to her two or three days later. God wanted to see what I would do. Would I still give, knowing that if I did I would not have enough to take care of the things that I needed to take care of? Would I be willing to trust God to provide what is missing? Or would I just not give? It is in this that you know what you're made of, whether you've grown spiritually or not, and if God is important to you.

I trusted God and I was not going to take my tithe money and give it for rent, no matter how short it was. If I did not pay my tithes and offering, I would have had enough to cover all the bills; but that would not have shown faith and trust in the God I serve. Paying your tithes and offering is a matter of the heart. Do you love God enough? Do you have that relationship with Him that no matter what you have or do not have you would still give the correct amount of your tithes to God? I'd rather be late paying my rent and pay the late fee than to not pay my tithes. God was merciful to me that the landlady did not charge me a late fee. Do not take your rent money to pay your tithes and offering, but you also should not take your tithes and offering to pay your rent. It's a test of how much you do love and trust God and how faithful you would be, believing that God would take care of everything. You will do as He says if you love Him. Watch Him work things out on your behalf. People do not understand the importance of paying tithes and offerings. It is vital to do so if you want God to bless you. Yes, you will lack some things in the beginning; but if you stick it out (which is very difficult to do), you will have more than you can handle. It is what He promised, and His promises are true.

You can also make God some of your own promises. Make sure you are faithful to whatever you have promised. God will honor you.

1. Make your promise.
2. Be faithful to your promise.
3. Work towards your promise.
4. Make sure you know and remember your promise so that you can fulfill what you have promised God.

God will always keep His promises to you and you need to always keep your promises to Him.

FIRST FRUITS

Tell the Israelites, when you have come into the land I give you and reap its harvest, you shall bring the sheaf of the first fruits of your harvest to the priest. (Leviticus 23:10)

The first fruits that God is speaking of here is not your entire earnings; it is still and always will be only ten percent of what you've made, or even received as a gift along with your free will offering. I have heard people say that your first fruit is all the money you've earned for the first week, or the month, but that is false. Yes, sometimes God will tell you or want you to put in an additional amount above your ten percent, to test you to see if you would give and be obedient, that's only because He has a specific blessing in mind for you. Yes, God will and can ask you for more because He asked me to give all I had. He will do that to you as well, and you will know when and what amount He wants you to give. We sometimes hear what God said to give (it is that very first amount that comes to you), and change our minds and give not a greater amount but a lesser amount. This is also disobedience. The first fruits of your income still are and forever will be the ten percent and your offerings are whatever you've decided to give. However, the more you do give, the more God will bless you. It is just how God works.

Your tithes and offerings are to be given to the pastor of your church. This means you give to the church in which you are a member. You are not really giving it to the pastors themselves, but for the functioning of the church. If you are a visitor, then you should give an offering. Do not ever go to church without giving something, and by that I mean even if it's a dime. The tithes and offering are to be brought every time that you get money.

1. Whether it's from a job.
2. If someone gives you money as a gift or inheritance.
3. If you get a loan from the bank.
4. If you get money to go to school.
   a. Such as financial aid.
   b. Such as a grant or a loan.
   c. Such as a scholar ship.

A tenth of that is for the Lord. I know some of you are saying that is all the people talk about at church, but if you would give God what He said to give, then they would not have to talk about it at church. You would or should have been grown up spiritually by now to pay your tithes. Don't worry of what another is doing, worry about yourself.

I have heard many pastors say that during the Summer time, the offerings are lower because people are going on vacation and they are not giving their tithes and offering. Now, how and why would you take what belongs to God and use it for your vacation? God is not pleased with that at all. In fact, He frowns on things like that. Do not take what belongs to God and do things that are not pleasing to God. Make sure that you do what God wants and you would have an even better vacation. God will allow you to have enough for your vacation if you would be faithful and give Him what belongs to Him.

God will not ask another if you have paid your tithes and offerings; He will ask you, and what would you say?

1. They were always talking about money and that's why I did not pay what You required me to do.
2. The pastor lived better than I did.
3. They did not need what little I had.
4. They had other people who can give.
5. I needed it more than You did.

It is a serious matter that needs to be addressed, and you need to stop making excuses and just do it. You are giving because God said so and because you love Him. When you give,

1. You do not give grudgingly.
2. You do not give sparingly.
3. You do not give meaninglessly.
4. You do not give with a mean spirit.

2 Corinthians 9:6-8 states:

> *[Remember] this: he who sows sparingly and grudgingly will also reap sparingly and grudgingly, and he who sows generously [that blessings may come to someone] will also reap generously and with blessings. Let each one give as he has made up in his own mind and purpose in his heart, not reluctantly or sorrowfully or under compulsion, for God loves (He takes pleasure in, prizes above other things, and is unwilling to abandon or to do without) a cheerful (joyous, prompt to do it) giver [whose heart is in his giving]. And God is able to make all grace (every favor and earthly blessing) come to you in abundance, so that you may always and under all circumstances and whatever the need be self-sufficient [possessing enough to require no aid or support and furnished in abundance for every good work and charitable donation].*

When you give, you must not only give out of your abundance but you must also give willingly. What will your harvest be if you give sparingly? What will you get back if you give grudgingly? What will your harvest be if you give generously? The word of God teaches us how to give. If you give a little you will get back little. If you give a lot you will get back a lot.

A few years ago when God told me to quit my job, I was a little worried because I had a house and all the bills that come with it, plus food and kids. When I finally obeyed, I felt a release. I felt pretty good. I had used up all my investments and had no more money, yet God was allowing all my bills to be paid and I was never late. This particular day I received a check in the mail for three thousand four hundred dollars, which I was never expecting; and as soon as I looked at it, in my mind I said, "I guess God wants me to give this away." But of course that quickly left my mind seeing I had need of it. I paid my tithes and offering right away because that was automatically God's, and I was not going to mess with that. That same week I was watching TBN and the person said to give one thousand dollars it would break the enemy's back. I went ahead and wrote a check and sent it off the next day. That evening, the same person came on again and said that it was double portion night send two thousand dollars so I said, "Well I guess You really wanted me to send this money after all." Although I had need of it, I wrote another check and sent it the very next day. See, it was the first thing that came to me and I had dismissed it. But God gave me another chance through TBN. Now I was broke and had no money. At least the three thousand dollars would and could have paid some bills; but it would have been for only that month, wherein, giving it to God would bring back a harvest that would bless me eventually. That month when my bills were due they were all paid by I don't know who or how, but it was only God who did it. For the rest of the months that I was there before I moved, God allowed all my bills to be paid and we were never hungry. In fact, we had food from a West Indian restaurant every day. I gave the money and forgot all about it, but once in a while it will come to my memory. You're probably saying, "But I do not have that kind of money." No, but you can give what you can. Mine was already in my heart to give, but the enemy quickly tried to take it away from me, but God sent another, to give me a second chance.

What's in your heart to give? Would you trust God and give Him what's in your hand?

In Mark 12:41-44 states:

And He (Jesus) sat down opposite the treasury and saw how the crowd was casting money into the treasury. Many rich [people] were throwing in large sums. And a widow who was poverty-stricken came and put in two copper mites [the smallest of coins], which together make half of a cent. And He called His disciples [to Him] and said to them truly and surely I tell you, this widow, [she who is] poverty-stricken, has put in more than all those contributing to the treasury. For they all threw in out of their abundance; but she, out of her deep poverty, has put in everything that she had—[even] all she had on which to live.

God promises some blessings. If we obey and give, He will in turn do some things for us.

1. The Lord will establish you.
2. You will defeat your enemies.
3. You shall be blessed in all that you do.
4. He will rebuke the devourer for your sake.

So you see it's not how much you give; it's what's in your heart when you give. Yes, God looks to see what you're putting in, but He's looking at your heart. Do not avoid giving because you don't think that you have enough to give; give what you have anyway.

One day I was watching TBN, and I saw a woman put twenty-seven cents on the altar. She was surely blessed that night. Everyone in the audience begin giving to her. Her purse could not hold the money that she was receiving and another tried to help collect the money that was falling to the ground. Did that blessing came because of how much she had given? No, it came because of her heart. Don't let these things stop you from giving. You never know when, where and how God is going to bless you. Things will never happen until you give. We need to give what we've got. We would never receive until we have given. Many of us do not like to give but we always need, and we always want something.

Deuteronomy 28:1-13 states:

If you will listen diligently to the voice of the Lord your God, being watchful to do all His commandments, which I command you this day, the Lord your God will set you high above all the nations of the earth. And all these blessings shall come upon you and over take you if you heed the voice of the Lord your God. Blessed shall you be in the city and blessed shall you be in the field. Blessed shall be the fruit of your body and the fruit of your ground and the fruit of your beasts, the increase of your cattle and the young of your flock. Blessed shall be your basket and your kneading trough. Blessed shall you be when you come in and blessed shall you be when you go out. The Lord shall cause your enemies who rise up against you to be defeated before your face; they shall come out against you one way and flee before you seven ways. The Lord shall command the blessing upon you in your storehouse and in all that you undertake. And He will bless you in the land which the Lord your God gives you. The Lord will establish you as a people holy to Himself, as He has sworn to you, if you keep the commandments of the Lord your God and walk in His ways. And all people of the earth shall see that you are called by the name [and in the presence of] the Lord, and they shall be afraid of you. And the Lord shall make you have a surplus of prosperity, through the fruit of your body, of your livestock and of your ground, in the land, which the Lord swore to your fathers to give you. The Lord shall open to you His good treasury, the heavens, to give the rain of your land in its season and to bless all the work of your hands, and you shall lend to many nations, but you shall not borrow. And the Lord shall make you the head, and not the tail; and you shall be above only, and you shall not be beneath, if you heed the commandments of the Lord your God which I command you this day and are watchful to do them.

The Lord repeated many times, if you would keep His commandments, He would do all these things that He swore to you. He will bless you immensely. He will always come through to His word, because He looks over His words to perform them. He will not fail you if you do your part.

Deuteronomy 8:18 states: *But you shall [earnestly] remember the Lord your God, for it is He who gives you power to get wealth that He may establish His covenant which He swore to your fathers, as it is this day.*

God may not give you money when you sow your seed (your tithes and offerings), but He will give it to you in writing a book, or inventing a product, or opening your own business. He will give you ideas of how to be successful; all you have to do is implement it.

I heard a story of a couple that were singers for the world making millions of dollars, and they became born-again believers. When they got saved they gave up everything; they had nothing. One of the record producers that worked with them told them that since they were in dire straits, they should or could make a million dollars with ease. All they had to do was just make one single record, but being true born-again believers, they said they would stick out what they were going through. When all hope was gone and they had not even a cent left and no job, God turned it around and blessed them.

You see; you could never out give God. They gave up millions, and we who have never even seen that much money cannot even give up a few pennies that we have. Everyone wants the blessings of God, but they do not want to bless God. Now, how many of you are true born-again believers? If you were, would you give up your last for God? We do not want to give up for God, but yet we expect to get from God. All you have to do is give God what belongs to Him and He will take care of what belongs to you.

CHAPTER 17
WITNESSING

Jesus said to go to the highways and byways and compel them to come. It is important that we share our salvation to those who are lost.

Luke 14:23 states:

> *Then the master said to the servant, go out into the highways and hedges and urge and constrain [them] to yield and come in, so that My house may be filled.*

When you develop a relationship with God, you will want to witness; you will have a desire for it. Why? It is the heart of Christ. You will just want to do it. God is about people and if He's in you, it will be your heart also.

2 Peter 3:9 states:

> *The Lord does not delay and is not tardy or slow about what He promises, according to some people's conception of slowness, but He is long-suffering (extraordinarily patient) toward you, not desiring that any should perish, but that all should come to repentance.*

It will not only be a pleasure to serve others, but it will also be pleasurable. You will not be able to wait to speak to someone about Christ, and what He's done for you, and what He will do for them. You will look to see and will say, who else can I be a blessing to? Who can I lend a helping hand to? Whom can I encourage today? You will always be on the lookout for someone you can be a blessing to.

WHY SHOULD YOU WITNESS?

We should witness because Jesus commanded us to do so. We were at one time lost, but now that we are saved we should want the world to be saved also. This was the reason Christ died to save the world from sin. We should have a desire to see the lost person found again.

Isaiah 53:6 states: *All we like sheep have gone astray, we have turn every one to his own way; and the Lord has made to light upon Him the guilt and iniquity of us all.*

This tells us that Jesus was coming to take upon Himself all of our sins and all of our iniquities in order to bring us back to God. It's like lost sheep that cannot find their way back to the Shepard; he has to go out and find them. The same thing Jesus has to do being our Shepard. He had to come and find us because we could never have found our way back to Him had He not come to find us. We should be willing, able, and ready to seek out those that Jesus said we should.

1. We have to seek out the lost sheep.
2. We have to seek out those that are sick.
3. We have to seek out the broken-hearted.
4. We have to seek out those who are imprisoned.

Ephesians 2:12 states:

[Remember] that you were at that time separated living apart) from Christ [excluded from all part in Him], utterly estranged and outlawed from the rights of Israel as a nation, and strangers with no share in the sacred compacts of the [Messianic] promise [with no knowledge of or right in God's agreements, His covenants]. And you had no hope (no promise); you were in the world without God.

Ephesians 4:18-19 states:

> *Their moral understanding is darkened and their reasoning is beclouded. [They are] alienated (estranged. Self-banished) from the life of God [with no share in it; this is] because of the ignorance (the want of knowledge and perception, the willful blindness) that is deep-seated in them, due to their hardness of heart [to the insensitiveness of their moral nature]. In their spiritual apathy they have become callous and pass feeling and reckless and have abandoned themselves [a prey] to unbridled sensuality, eager and greedy to indulge in every form of impurity [that their depraved desires may suggest and demand].*

Acts 1:8 states:

> *But you shall receive power (ability, efficiency, and might) when the Holy Spirit has come upon you, and you shall be My witnesses in Jerusalem and all Judea and Samaria and to the ends (the very bounds) of the earth.*

We are to go and do as Jesus said. We all may not be able to witness any further than our neighbor hoods; but we must certainly go and tell others about the love of God and of His precious Son. We can also give to other ministries that are reaching out to lost souls all over the nation, such as TBN.

HOW SHOULD WE WITNESS?

We should witness with all meekness. We should humble ourselves. Not having overcome certain things does not give you the right to judge those people to whom you are witnessing, and who have not yet overcome their struggles and situations. Not because it was easy for you to overcome certain issues means that it's easy for them to overcome theirs. You may have gone through the same things, but everyone has their own way of overcoming; so please do not judge or condemn those people who still struggle with theirs. It does not give you the right to judge or to criticize them. If you're spiritual you should:

1. Be able to speak to someone in love.
2. Be able to speak to someone in meekness.
3. Be able to speak to someone with sensitivity.
4. Be able to speak to someone in a nonjudgmental way.

You should always be nice to those to whom you're witnessing. You do not want to tell the person, "Don't do as I do; do as I say." The people are looking at your life, so let it be an example and they will want to follow you. Remember, it is Jesus Christ you're representing. He gives us ways in which He wants us to respond to others, and we must follow and adhere to His guidelines.

Galatians 6:1 states:

> *Brethren, if any person is overtaken in misconduct or sin of any sort, you who are spiritual [who are responsive to and controlled by the Spirit] should set him right and restore and reinstate him, without any sense of superiority and with all gentleness, keeping an attentive eye on yourself, less you should be tempted also.*

Always speak to others without judgment. These are some ways how to speak with those with whom you come in contact that you want to witness to.

1. Be loving and compassionate.
2. Listen to what they are saying.
3. Speak softly and tenderly (do not shout or raise your voice).

4. Do not cut them off while they are speaking.
5. Make sure they repeat the sinner's prayer.
6. Make sure you pray for them before leaving.

These things will make the other person open up to you and not be afraid to speak what's on their mind and of what's bothering them.

1 Corinthians 10:12 states: *Therefore let anyone who thinks he stands [who feels sure that he has a steadfast mind and is standing firm], take heed lest he fall [into sin].*

Do not think too highly of yourself because you have overcome some things and another has not. Do not be too hasty to point a finger to those that God is working on.

WITNESSING IN DIFFICULT TIMES

Many days you will not feel like witnessing. You might be feeling sick that day, or someone may have upset you. Or you just don't feel like being bothered. That's when you should want to go the most because the enemy is trying to stop you from being a blessing to someone who might even be a blessing to you. Sometimes you have to press your way through. Don't let the enemy stop you from getting and receiving what God has for you because you're not in the mood. Sometimes you go out to witness and there's nobody there to witness to. What do you do then? Do you sulk and go back home or do you go to another spot? Do you say, "Well, I guess God does not want me to do this today?" Or do you stay a while and see if someone will show up? Jesus waited for the woman of Samaria. You must be able to:

1. Sit and wait, being patient in your work.
2. Shake off all manner of sicknesses that the enemy tries to bring your way.

3. Do not be so easily willing to give up because you do not feel up to par.
4. Do not think that what you're doing is a waste of time.
    a. Because you have to stop what you're doing to witness.
    b. Because it cuts into your lunchtime.
    c. Because it takes time away from what you want to do.
    d. Because it takes time away from your family.

God will restore the time and the years back to you if you're faithful in what you do.

John 4:3-9 states:

> *He (Jesus) left Judea and returned to Galilee. It was necessary for Him to go through Samaria. And in doing so, he arrived at a Samaritan town called Sychair, near the tract of land that Jacob gave to his son Joseph. And Jacob's well was there. So Jesus, tired as He was from His journey, sat down [to rest] by the well. It was then about the sixth hour (about noon). Presently, when a woman of Samaria came along to draw water, Jesus said to her, give Me a drink-for His disciples had gone off into the town to buy food. The Samaritan woman said to Him, how is it that you being a Jew, ask me, a Samaritan [and a] woman, for a drink-for the Jews had nothing to do with the Samaritans.*

Jesus knew exactly when the woman would come to draw water, for it was her habit to do so at that time. Jesus reached there before she got there and waited for her. He was not too proud to ask a woman whom the Jews did not speak to for some water. This was His opening to minister to her. She considered Jacob her father just as the Jews considered Abraham their father. They were related and did not even know or did not care. The Jews thought they were too good for them. God Almighty always introduces Himself saying, "I Am the God of Abraham, Isaac, and [who? Yes,] Jacob." Jesus had a mission and it had to be fulfilled. Do not let anyone make you feel like you're wasting your time because you're not. You are helping God to perform the things He needs in order for one to come to salvation. When they try to tell you what you should and should not do, do not listen to them. Walk away from them. Do not respond to them. Ignore any remarks that they may say, and do not give up.

Verses 27-34 states:

> *Just then His disciples came and they wondered (were surprised, astonished) to find Him talking with a woman [a married woman], however, not one of them asked Him, what are you inquiring about? Or what do you want? Or, why do you speak with her? Then the woman left her water jar and went away to the town. And she began telling the people, come, see a Man who has told me everything that I ever did! Can this be [is not this] the Christ? [must not this be the Messiah, The Anointed One?] So the people left the town and set out to go to Him. Meanwhile, the disciples urged Him saying, Rabbi, eat something. But He assured them, I have food (nourishment) to eat of which you know nothing and have no idea. So the disciples said one to another, has someone brought Him something to eat? Jesus said to them, My food (nourishment) is to do the will (pleasure) of Him who sent Me and to accomplish and completely finish His work.*

Jesus made a disciple out of the woman by her telling all in town what He had told her. She no longer wanted water from just any well, but water from His well, which is the living water that will flow out of your bellies. The people urged Jesus to stay and He did for two days. How long do you want Jesus to stay? In fact, do you get up after praying right away or do you wait to hear what He has to say? After all the words and things you've talked to Him about, you need to take the time to listen to what He has to say regarding what you've just prayed about. Jesus' disciples wondered why He spoke to the woman and would have turned her away (just like church folk). You never know:

1. If you'll make a disciple out of that person.
2. If you would lead them to Christ.
3. If they would turn around and be a blessing to you.
4. If they would be the one God uses to change and impact the world or even the nations.

It always comes from those that you least expect. Do not overlook anyone because of how they are right now. God does not see what they are; God sees what they will become. God speaks to them about where they are going and not where they are. God knows what He has planted inside of you. That's to be what He wants, and has called and designed you to be.

Philippians 3:14 states: *I press on toward the goal to win the [supreme and heavenly] prize to which God in Christ Jesus is calling us upward.* When you press towards what God has for you He will reward you with things that you least expect. He will even give you things that you did not ask for.

A PRIZE TO BE WON

There is a prize to be won if you do not let how you feel affect what you do. There will be times you are not able to make it, but if you can help it, try to make it out, even if it's to one person. That might just be the one God had ordained to be a blessing to you that day because of your faithfulness and determination. These are a few obstacles that may come your way that those you try to witness too might say.

1. Christian people are hypocrites.
2. All the pastor wants is your money.
3. I do not have to go to church.
4. I can worship at home.
5. The people at church talked about me.
6. I see people who are in church doing the same things and going to the same places that I do.
7. Why should I go to church?
8. I've tried that route before and it did not work for me.
9. People who I see go to church are mean.
10. They're all faking.
11. God does not exist.

What would you say to these people? Do you know your word enough to answer these questions? Would you get nervous if these questions came up? Which one would you not want to come up in conversation? When you are out in the world to point the way to Christ, these obstacles and more could come up against you and the one you hate the most to come up maybe the very one that will come up. So familiarize yourself with what you want to talk about and foresee any obstacles that may come your way. In other words, think ahead. You must be aware of what they will say to you and what you will say to them and how to say it in love. You must season your speech with salt and be easily ready to give them an answer of the hope that lies within you. You must tell them the "whys" you are the way you are and the reason behind what you do.

1. Why you want to suffer for Christ?
2. Why you wanted to accept Christ?
3. Why you still serve Him after the hardship you've been through?
4. Why God did not let the enemy wipe you out?
5. Why you have overcome and got the victory?

You must freely and openly discuss some of the things that you have gone through. Let them know that they are not the only one that bad things have happened to, and so that they can see God's grace and mercy.

2 Timothy 2:3 states: *Take [with me] your share of the hardships and suffering [which you are called to endure] as a good [first-class] solder of Christ Jesus.*

Being a good witness means you will suffer many things. The devil does not want you to witness to others because he will be losing those to whom you've witnessed too quickly; he will put stumbling blocks in your way. Do not let that get you down; just thank God that the enemy is scared of you, which is why he's giving you such a difficult time. You have power in God. Use it. Tap into what God has for you. You can only do this through praying, fasting and meditating on God's word.

1 Peter 4:16 states: *But if [one is ill-treated and suffers] as a Christian [which he is contemptuously called], let him not be ashamed, but give glory to God that he is [deemed worthy to suffer] in this name.*

Do not ever be ashamed of God and the things that He has allowed you to go through in order for you to grow and be like Jesus Christ. It is a blessing to be able to witness to those that are lost and for you to walk them through the process of receiving salvation. God will use you more and in a larger and higher capacity when and if you do the smaller things now. God will reward you for your hard work and your faithfulness; and remember according to Proverbs, "He that winneth souls is wise." So go out there and win souls for Christ.

CHAPTER 18
PRAYER

I have heard people say, "You only get what you need when you pray, not what you want." You will always get whatever you pray for once it's in the will of God, whether it's what you need or what you want.

John 2:3 states: *And when they wanted wine, the mother of Jesus saith unto Him, they have no wine. (KJV)*

This scripture states that they wanted wine, not that they needed it because if you read the text it was way towards the end of the wedding when Jesus gave them six water pots full of new wine (that was about twenty to thirty gallons per water pot). God is the one who decides what we need and what we don't. He will give you in overflow. Some people say it does not matter how you pray, but that's not the case.

The Bible says in James 5:16: *The effectual fervent prayer of a righteous man availeth much. (KJV)*

People use this verse without even knowing what it means. What does that mean (the effectual fervent prayer)?

Effectual means legally valid, or binding as an agreement.

Fervent means showing great intensity of feeling, a burning.

Intensity means the strength or degree of force with which something is done.

This means that you pray with everything you've got inside of you. Knowing this, where do you see that it does not matter how you pray?

BE PERSISTENT

There are criteria that we have to follow in order for God to move on our behalf. We must never stray away from them because they are vital for our prayers being answered.

1. We must ask according to His will.
2. We must ask continuously and consistently.
3. We must never give up.
4. We must be in relationship with God.

There are a few things that we must do when we want God to do what we are asking Him for. There are guidelines and a way of doing things to please God. You cannot come to God any old way and expect Him to move on your behalf or expect Him to jump at your request because you are in a bind and need to get out as quickly as possible. It does not work that way; it is always and forever will be in God's timing. You may think that you need that thing like yesterday. God knows exactly when you really do need it and He will give it to you at the appropriate and appointed time. God is the One that places the desires in your heart. You then have a need to pray for what's in your heart. You then have to be patient for that thing to come about and you have to believe that you have received it. While you're waiting, you need to give God praise and thanks that He has heard you and will answer you. We must not be in too much of a hurry to get what we want. We should be willing and ready to wait for it. How much do you want what you're asking God for? You will end up trying to help God or you might even give up on God if you cannot wait. You would end up being even more miserable than you were before, and you will also be in a worse place than you've ever been.

1. Be willing to be persistent.
2. Be willing to go out of your way.
3. Be willing to wait.

WHAT'S THE PRICE FOR YOUR SOUL?

4. Be willing to hear no.
5. Be willing to go back again.

If you're willing to do these things, you will gain the things that God has for you. There's a story that I like about a widow and a judge and if you're persistent you will get what you want.

Luke 18:1-8 states:

> *Also [Jesus] told them a parable to the effect that they ought always to pray and not to turn coward (faint, lose heart, and give up). He said, in a certain city there was a judge who neither reverenced and feared God nor respected or considered man. And there was a widow in that city who kept coming to him and saying, protect and defend and give me justice against my adversary. And for a time he would not; but later he said to himself, thought I have neither reverence or fear for God nor respect or consideration for man, yet because this widow continues to bother me, I will defend and protect and avenge her, lest she give me intolerable annoyance and wear me out by her continual coming or at the last she come and rail on me or assault me or strangle me. Then the Lord said, listen to what the unjust judge says! And will not [our just] God defend and protect and avenge His elect (His chosen ones), who cry to Him day and night? Will He defer them and delay help on their behalf? I tell you, He will defend and protect and avenge them speedily. However, when the Son of Man comes, will He find [persistence in] faith on the earth?*

God will always do things to show you that He cares and that He is right there for you.

1. God will protect you.
2. God will avenge you.
3. God will not delay to help you.

191

4. God will not defer to be a blessing to you.

If we do not give up we would always get what we want. Although God bears long with us, it does not mean that He does not want us to have what we are asking for. It simply means that we should persevere the more and with more patience while we wait on God. God taking long to answer is not necessarily a no; it just might be that it's not time to receive that thing in which we are asking Him for. We do not like waiting; we want everything quick, easy and in a hurry. God does not work that way all the time, He likes to see how much you do want that thing and how important it is to you, how much patience you have and what you are willing to go through for it.

Remember the woman Jesus called a dog? Why did He call her a dog? What did she do when He called her a dog? Did she leave without her blessing? Let's find out. If you're ashamed, then things will not happen for you. Are you ashamed to beg? Are you ashamed to keep going back? Are you ashamed to worship? Are you ashamed to put aside your pride? Are you ashamed that your feelings might be hurt? Our feelings get hurt from time to time, but you need not be ashamed of the things that you may have to go through.

1. Going through helps us to come out stronger than we went in.
2. Going through gives us the strength to go through again.
3. Going through shows God that we are willing to do whatever it is that He wants.
4. Going through shows our determination for that thing.

Matthew 15:21-28 states:

> *And going away from there, Jesus withdrew to the district of Tyre and Sidon. And behold a woman who was a Canaanite from that district came out and, with a [loud, troublesomely urgent] cry, begged, have mercy on me, O Lord, son of David! My daughter is miserably and distressingly and cruelly possessed by a demon! But He did not answer her a word. And His disciples came and implored Him, saying; send her away, for she is crying out after us. He (Jesus) answered, I was sent only to the lost sheep of the house of Israel. But she came, and kneeling, worshiped Him and kept praying, Lord, help me. And He answered, it is not right (proper, becoming, or fair) to take the children's bread and throw it to the little dogs. She said, yes, Lord, yet even the little pups eat the crumbs that fall from their (young) masters' table. Then Jesus answered her, O woman, great is your faith! Be it done for you as you wish. And her daughter was cured from that moment.*

What would you have done? Would you have walked away? Jesus called her a dog because in those days we all were considered dogs that were outside the Jewish faith. Healing, Jesus said, was the children's bread and was not given to an outsider. Did the woman give up? The woman yet worshipped Him and admitted that she was a dog. Nonetheless, could you please still help me? And because of her persistence, she went away with her blessing because Jesus healed her daughter.

Many of us would have given up. Our pride would have stood in the way of our blessing and our feelings would have been hurt and we would have walked away from the name-calling. I know I would. I am the kind of person if I ask you for something once with me knowing that you can do it (that's why I'm asking in the first place) and you turned me down; trust me, I would never ask you for anything ever again even if my life depended on it. When it comes to God I will beg, scream, cry, and even holler until He shows up. He can call me whatever He wants to. He could even spit on me, I just won't care. That did not stop this woman. She was desperate for a miracle. How desperate are you? How badly do you want your blessing? What are you willing to do for it? Whatever you put into your prayer life, that is what you will get out of it.

1. Do you put God first?
2. Do you put other things first?
   a. Your cars.
   b. Your home.
   c. Your money and your bling, bling.
   d. Your love life.
3. Do you put your children first?
4. Do you put your spouse first?
5. Do you put other people first?
   a. Friends
   b. Co-Workers
   c. Those in need
   d. Mother and Father
   e. Brothers and Sisters

All those people have their place in your life and yes, you should help and be a blessing to them; however, God should and must always be number one priority in your life. You should always put Him first in all that you do and above anyone even those in need. When you do you will be better able and better equipped to serve those in need.

My grandmother told me that many years ago when she was young in her early thirties, she would always try to get her kitchen clean and in order before she goes to pray because it would be on her mind so she would only pray for fifteen minutes a day. Then one day she heard a voice that said, "That's all you're going to get." My grandmother said she knew exactly what that meant. Since she was only giving God fifteen minutes of her time then only fifteen minutes He (God) was going to give her back. From that day on, my grandmother said she prayed and praised Him at least an hour every day. You see, the more you pray the more He will give back to you.

God wants us to pray and the enemy wants us not to. The enemy knows that when and if we pray we loose Gods' hand to bless us and he (the devil) does not want us to be blessed. God knows that when you do what He wants, He will eventually release what it is that He has in His hands for you.

1 Thessalonians 5:17 states: *Be unceasing in prayer [praying perseveringly]*.

That means that you are to pray every day without skipping. God must consistently be on your mind. Pray and read your bible every day. Some of us give up just as we're at or on the verge of our breakthrough. That's when the enemy fights us the most. That's our clue to press on even harder, to pray even more vigorously. To get what you want from God, you have to be willing to go after it with all you've got. The enemy does not want us to be blessed or even to be happy, but he can never stop God from doing what God said He would do.

The key is for you not to give up or back off because adversity is in your way (the devil is a liar). God is a God of His word. That is why we have to keep praying until our blessing comes. Our continuous prayers give the angels strength to fight our battles. Daniel prayed 21 days before his answer came. Why? God had already sent an angel to give Daniel the answer that he was seeking. His prayer lasted for 21 days because there was a wrestling match going on in the heavenly realm with the devil and the angel that God had sent. Michael, the archangel, had to take over the other angel's position fighting with the devil as the angel with the message for Daniel escaped to give Daniel the message from God. If you need or want anything, then you need to get on your face before God.

BE CAREFUL WHO YOU ALLOW TO PRAY FOR YOU

You need to be careful whom you let pray for you. There are people who put God in a box and do not believe as you do. One day, my former pastor came to my home and wanted to pray for me. His prayer was, "Lord please send her a husband that will help her pay the mortgage." There is nothing wrong with that prayer, but he just limited what I want God to do in my life. I was surprised because I did not need any man to help me with any such thing. What I wanted God to do for me was nothing materialistic. It was spiritual; and no mere man could do those things for me. Since then I never let him pray for me anymore because what I wanted and what he wanted for me were two different things. He thought that since I was single and had no job, I needed help. He just did not see or understand how all of my bills were being paid so that was his prayer. Which one do you think God would answer? God said that if two will agree on touching anything, He would do it. Well, the pastor and I were not in agreement. God does not answer anything contrary to what the individual wants. For instance, if someone is married and wanted a divorce and somebody comes along and prays for that person to get back together with their spouse, which one would God answer? God, of course, would answer the one who wants a divorce. God would not give you something that you do not want. If God wants you to have it, He would give you a liking for it. Do not let anyone put your God in his or her little box. You put God in your own box. Yours might just be bigger than the other person's box. We however should take God out of the box but some of us; our faith is not that high as yet. We have to work towards that level.

God knows what we have need of even before we know, and if you do not ask for yourself you might not get what God has for you. Do not give it over to someone else to pray for you, they will, and might pray for things that are not high enough for you. They might just ask God to give you a regular house when God has a mansion for you. Jesus said to ask and it shall be given unto you. He also said that you have not because you ask not and we should ask that our joy might be full. So think big when you pray because God said, "As high as the heaven is from the earth are His ways and thoughts higher than ours."

1. Are you willing to cry out to God?
2. Are you willing not to listen to people?
3. Are you willing to wait all day on your face if you had to?
4. Are you willing to throw off the old you?

Mark 10:46-51 states:

Then they came to Jericho, and as they He was leaving Jericho with His disciples and a great crowd, Bartimaeus, a blind beggar, a son of Timaeus, was sitting by the roadside. And when he heard that it was Jesus of Nazareth, he began to shout, saying, Jesus, Son of David, have pity and mercy on me [now]. And many severely censured and reproved him, telling him to keep still, but he kept on shouting out all the more, you Son of David have pity and mercy on me [now]. And Jesus stopped and said, call him and they called the blind man, telling him, take courage! Get up! He (Jesus) is calling you. And throwing off his outer garment, he leaped up and came to Jesus. And Jesus said to him, what do you want Me to do for you? And the blind man said to Him, Master, let me receive my sight.

Persistence is the key to your unanswered prayers. Blind Bartimaeus (as we like to call him) was irritating the people around him with the noise that he was making and so they tried to shut him up. Do not let anyone stop you from reaching God. When you reach Him, He might surprise you and turn around and ask you a question. Make sure you know exactly what it is that you want before you call on Him. How desperate are you? What are you willing to go through? How long would you wait for your prayers to be answered? If you are persistent enough you will be blessed. So you see it does matter how long you pray and how you pray. If it were not important, it would not be written in the bible.

1. You have to be passionate.
2. You have to be consistent.
3. You have to be forceful.
4. You have to be able to make something happen.

You need to put your heart into all that you do for God. You have to go after what He said with enthusiasm.

Matthew 11:12 states:

> *And from the days of John the Baptist until the present time, the kingdom of heaven has endured violent assault, and violent men seize it by force [as a precious prize-a share in the heavenly kingdom is sought with most ardent zeal and intense exertion].*

To get what you want from God, you have to be willing to go after it with all you've got. By that I mean to fall on your face and seek God with all your heart, and want Him and Him alone. You also need to fast and pray.

FASTING AND PRAYING

You're probably wondering what is fasting and why do you need to fast and pray? Well, let's see what it means to fast.

Fasting-According to us (Christians) as believers implies total abstinence from all foods or something that you like to do for a certain period of time. The length of time varies. It could be anytime and any day of your choice. It also helps to flush out your system. It is a time of consecration to the Lord and a time that you dedicate to Him. We fast for many reasons.

1. To get the strongholds off of us.
2. To get God to intervene and show up on our behalf.
3. To get much closer to God and His anointing.
4. To get more spiritual and to gain spiritual things.
5. To overcome our adversary.

When you fast, you have to pray and read your bible during the fasting period, usually more often than when you're not on a fast. The reason for fasting is to be able to kill all those strongholds on your life. All those things that seem to have more control of you than you have of it. You also get closer to God and a better relationship with Him. You cannot fast without praying but you can pray without fasting.

And when they had ordained them elders in every church, and had prayed with fasting, they commended them to the Lord, on whom they believed. (Acts 14:23)

While they were worshiping the Lord and fasting, the Holy Spirit said, separate now for Me Barnabas and Saul for the work to which I have called them. Then after fasting and praying, they put their hands on them and sent them away. (Acts 13:2-3)

Do not refuse and deprive and defraud each other [of your due marital rights], except perhaps by mutual consent for a time, so that you may devote yourselves unhindered to prayer. But afterwards resume material relations, lest Satan tempt you [to sin] through your lack of restrain of sexual desires. (1 Corinthians 7:5)

There are many different kinds of fasts. There is a forty day fast. There is a thirty day fast. There is a twenty-one day fast. There is a fourteen day fast. There is a seven day fast. There is a three day fast. There is a twenty-four hour fast and there is a twelve-hour fast. Any time you want to fast, it's all up to you to decide the days and times and hours that you want. There are many more you can do. You chose how many days you can handle. Fasting does not only pertain to not eating but you can also fast from talking on the phone and from watching television.

Forty Day Fast

Jesus fasted forty days in the wilderness before He started His ministry and was also tempted by the enemy.

Then Jesus was led (guided) by the [Holy] Spirit into the wilderness (desert) to be tempted (tested and tried) by the devil. And He went without food for forty days and forty nights, and later He was hungry. (Matt. 4:1-2)

When you are fasting for forty days, you have to be careful and make sure that God placed you on it because it could make you ill. When you're doing such a long fast you need to make sure that you are not overworking yourself and make sure you get plenty of rest.

Thirty Day Fast

There is no recorded thirty day fast in the bible; however, many people today fast for thirty days because they feel the need to go for a month. In most cases, when people are doing this fast they do eat but mostly fruits and vegetables or they eat no desserts for that month. Going on a fast for thirty days, you also have to be careful because you can also become dehydrated. Pray before going on any long fast and make sure you're doing it for God and not just to lose weight.

Twenty-One Day Fast

This fast is most popular. Every year, beginning the first month of the year, myself and many others such as Jensen Franklin go on a straight twenty one days, seven days a week without eating or taking a break. This is called the Daniel fast.

In those days I, Daniel, was mourning for three whole weeks. I ate no pleasant or desirable food, nor did any meat or wine come into my mouth; and I did not anoint myself at all for the full three weeks. On the twenty-fourth day of the first month, as I was on the bank of the great river Hiddekel [which is the Tigris] I lifted up my eyes and looked, and behold, a man clothed in linen, whose loins were girded with pure gold of Uphaz. (Daniel 10:2-3)

And behold, a hand touched me, which set me [unsteadily] upon my knees and upon the palms of my hands. And [the angel] said to me, O Daniel, you greatly beloved man, understand the words that I speak to you and stand upright, for to you I am now sent. And while he was saying this word to me, I stood up trembling. Then he said to me, Fear not, Daniel, for from the first day that you set your mind and heart to understand and to humble yourself before your God, your words were heard, and I have come as a consequence of [and in response to] your words. But the prince of the kingdom of Persia withstood me for twenty-one days. Then Michael, one of the chief [of the celestial] princes, came to help me, for I remained there with the kings of Persia. (Daniel 10:13)

Fourteen-Day Fast

While they waited until it should become day, Paul entreated them all to take some food, saying, This is the fourteenth day that you have been continually in suspense and on the alert without food, having eaten nothing. (Acts 27:33)

There is a two weeks fast that you can go on. During the year, I've been on a few of these. I see the difference it made in my life. Fasting for two weeks is not easy, but it can get you to that place in God that you're striving to be.

Seven Day Fast

The week fast most people can handle. It is a fast that has a significant meaning. Seven is God's favorite number. Many men and women of God when they are going through some things and need God's response, they go on the seven-day fast. I also went on this fast for God to change some things in my oldest son's life. After this fast, God actually did what I asked of Him.

Three Day Fast

The three-day fast is considered the Esther fast. She fasted to get God to intervene on the behalf of His people.

Go, gather together all the Jews that are present in Shushan, and fast for me; and neither neither eat nor drink for three days, night or day. I also and my maids will fast as you do.

*Then I will go to the king, though it is against the law; and if
I perish, I perish. (Esther 4:16)*

Twenty Four Hour Fast

The twenty-four hour fast is normally from sunset to sunset. It
is a fast to quickly go to God and prostrate before Him and tell
Him of all your needs and of all your concerns. When you do,
you will see that God will move quickly on your behalf.

Twelve Hour Fast

The twelve-hour fast is the sun up to sun down or it can be any
time of the day that you choose. This is not too bad. You have
to start somewhere and you have to try your best to want to put
off the things that have you bound. By starting here, you will see
that you can and will become stronger each and every time you
fast.

Keep in mind that when you fast you have to also keep away
from any sexual contact with your spouse. You have to remain
pure and be purified. When you're fasting, it is your choice
what you decide to do. You can choose your own days and how
you want it to go. For example, you may want to only go a day
without television or half a day with no food and no telephone.
It's all up to you.

*And the Lord said to Moses, Go and sanctify the people [set
them apart for God] today and tomorrow, and let them wash
their cloths.(Exodus 19:10)*

*And Moses went down from the mount unto the people, and
sanctified the people; and they washed their clothes. And he
said unto the people, be ready against the third day; come not
at your wives.(Exodus 19:14-15 KJV)*

If it is your first time fasting, you need to start out small such as maybe start with an hour or two before you jump into a three-day or a seven-day fast. You also should not mix talking on the phone if you can help it, and lessen your TV intake. Maybe you might even want to start by pushing one meal away and you may start with the one you love the most. You should always do a sacrificial fast. It should be something that you want that is why you're giving it up, that is what pleases God. Going on any fast is not easy. As soon as you declare that you will be fasting, all-of-a-sudden, you will start feeling hungry. When you're not on a fast, you can go all day without eating. However, as soon as you say that you are going to push your plate back, you feel like you're going to pass out from hunger. It's all in your mind. Every food place you pass by smells good and everything regarding food you see looks good. Even if you do not eat that particular item, it still looks good and smells good.

When you're going through your fast you need to make sure you drink plenty of water, which also helps to flush your system out. You may also drink fruit juices and not sodas if it's liquids only. This is what we should do on our fast; however, some people work long hours and cannot go for twenty fours hours for twenty-one days. In this case, you need to eat lightly, mostly fruits and vegetables and make sure that you do not eat any desserts.

When you finally come off the fast, you have to make sure that you do not overeat because it will happen and you will feel that you were deprived and try to make up for it. When you first get off the fast, drink some soup and do not add too much salt because in most cases your taste buds will not work for a while especially if you went on a long fast. When you focus yourself on God and God alone and you read your word, fast, and pray, God will become not only your Father but He will be your friend. God and you will be inseparable. You will have that deep intimacy, that deep passion for Him. As you keep on praying and reading your word, you get closer every time and in due season you will see that after a while, God will give you what's in His hand.

CHAPTER 19
BEING TIRED OF WHAT YOU DO

When you are working in a ministry and you feel like your work is a drag, or you're volunteering in many aspects of the church and you feel like giving up, or you no longer want to do what you're doing; you need to stop; you may be in the wrong line of work or you may have bitten off more than you can chew. Meaning, it's not your assignment from God and you've put yourself in that position. If the position was put there by yourself; then yes, you will get tired and fed-up with it and you'll think that something is wrong with you. You'll even work harder not realizing that it's not your assignment.

Mark 4:38 states: *But He [Himself] was in the stern [of the boat], a sleep on the [leather] cushion; and they awoke Him and said to Him, Master, do you not care that we are perishing?*

Yes, Jesus became very tired and sleepy, but He never got tired and fed up with what He was doing. Once you live in this body, you will get tired but getting tired with what you're doing is a sure sign that you're taking on too much and you need to cut back. Don't over-do it. It will wear you out. Take a good look at what it is that God said, and what it is that you are doing. Are these things a match? If not, then you need to start all over and do only what God said that you should do. These are things that can cause a person to turn mean and bitter, especially when they do not like what they are doing. They have no sense of fulfillment and they're running around like a chicken that has lost its head.

Yes, doing God's work sometimes gets hectic and overwhelming. Yes, you do get tired because your body could only take so much and no more before it starts to break down. Even Jesus was tired and sat by the well; that's because He walked just about everywhere He went. These days we have buses, trains, cars, and planes to take us where we want to go. The reality is that most people are doing things not because God told them to, but because of their own agenda. What is the real reason you're doing what you do?

1. Are you doing these things to be seen?
2. Are you doing these things to get attention?
3. Are you doing these things because it's your real assignment?
4. Are you doing these things to impress someone?

What is the purpose behind what you do? What drives you? In other words, what motivates you to do what you do? I know that God did not tell you to take on all that you are taking on. Why push your body to the limit like that? When you die, God will use someone else to take your place. What I mean is? God will never tell you to push yourself to death. He's not that kind of God. He wants us to take a break. So back to the question, what is driving you to do what you do?

I know of a few pastors who brag about staying in fancy hotels when they travel and all the glamour that comes with it; and how they are catered to hand and foot. Do you ask God what assignment to take? Or do you just take it because of how much it pays? God might not have wanted you to take that particular assignment. He might have wanted you to take a different one, but because it did not pay as much as the other, you turned it down. God wants everyone who is working for Him to acknowledge Him in everything that they do; including asking Him which assignment He wants you to go on. People take assignments for many reasons on their own, and then their bodies become sick, tired, and malnourished and they wonder, if they're doing God's work why this is happening to them. But did you include God in what you say is His work? You need to inquire of God what it is that He wants you to do.

1. Ask God, is this what you want me to do.
2. Ask God if you should go.
3. Ask God where you should go.
4. Ask God, what do you want me to say?
5. Ask God if this pleases Him.

Do not let what Christ did for you go in vain. Although you may be doing His work, whether it's preaching, teaching, ministering, prophesying, volunteering or whatever the case may be. I know that you know that only what you do for God will last; but it can also be in vain if your heart is not in the right place with Him. Besides, it's not by works anyways, lest any man should boast, according to Ephesians 2:9. Sometimes we can be so busy doing God's work that we forget to or have no time to spend with who we are working for, which is God. Yes, only what you do for Him will last, but what is the reason behind what you're doing? Is it for money? Is it for fame? Is it to be noticed? Is it for God? What is the reason you do what you do? There is always a reason and if you would be honest with yourself, the truth will come out. If it is not a good reason, you still have a chance to change it and to ask God to forgive you. It's better to know the truth than to lie to yourself. And when you die God puts you on His left side and tell you to depart form Him, those who worked iniquity. It will be too late then to ask His forgiveness.

Many people in that day will be on their knees asking (begging) for forgiveness and making all manner of excuses, but it will fall on deaf ears. God will not hear you. You will say, "But God, I was doing your work and many a day I was exhausted. How can this be? Many people got saved. Many of them got blessed. Why are you doing this to me?" He will reply,

1. You may have been doing work for Me, but it was to get praise from people.

2. You may have been doing work for Me, but it was for the money.
3. You may have been doing work for Me, but you did not treat your neighbors right.
4. You may have been doing work for Me, but you did not visit those in prison.
5. You may have been doing work for Me, but you did not treat the little children right.
6. You may have been doing work for Me, but you forgot to include Me.
7. You were not actually doing work for Me; you were doing it for yourself.

It could be a whole array of things. Be true to yourself now and save your soul in the long run, than to lie to yourself and damn your soul to hell. Why wait until that day to hear Him say these things to you? Make sure that you are doing it for the right reasons now, than have to hear Him say it to you in that day.

In 1 Corinthians 9:27 Paul states:

> *But [like a boxer] I buffet my body [handle it roughly, discipline it by hardships] and subdue it, for fear that after proclaiming to others the Gospel and things pertaining to it, I myself should become unfit [not stand the test, be unapproved and rejected as a counterfeit].*

You have to be careful because just as quickly and as easily as you rise to the top, it can all get to your head and you can fall to the ground just as easily.

Zechariah 7:5-6 states:

> *Speak to all the people of the land and to the priests, saying, when you fasted and mourned in the fifth and seventh months,*

even those seventy years you were in exile, was it for Me that you fasted, for Me? and when you eat and when you drank, did you not eat for yourselves and drink for yourselves?

You have to make sure you're doing the things that you are meant to do. Check to make sure that you're doing things of God for the right reasons. When you're doing the work that you say is God's work, make sure you ask yourself these questions.

1. Did I do it for God?
2. Did I do it for the money?
3. Did I do it to be seen?
4. Did I do it for His glory?

Many of us do not want to ask God what He would have us to do. We just assume that since it is preaching, teaching, ministering that this is His work and we need not ask His opinion. So we weary ourselves, even working with pain saying, "I'm doing this for God;" but in reality you are doing it for yourselves. These are some of the things I know that some; not all, preachers, pastors, evangelists, bishops and all the others who say they work for the Lord are really going after these things and their heart is not for God but for whatever they can get. These may be some of the reasons why you do what you do.

1. You're doing it to be noticed.
2. You're doing it to be popular.
3. You're doing it for the fame.
4. You're doing it to get your name out there.
5. You're doing it to make a legacy.

The more you do, the more people will see you and recognize you and call out your name and you become famous like a movie star and all this gets to your head. If you're trying to leave a legacy, it will not work if God is not in it. You will work yourself to death and you still will not obtain.

What message are we sending the next generation? They see all the big mansions and fancy cars, all the glitz and glamour and they want to be like that. They're not saying I want the God that's in that person. They just want the material things. Serving the Lord after going through a while, you do end up with these material things, because God will not allow you to go through without giving you things in return. They first got the spiritual things. Then God blesses them and they can do whatever they want with it; but it came with a price. You cannot just look at the big time preachers and say you want what they have without first wanting what they also suffered in order to receive what God has blessed them with. Do not look at the material things. Look for God to give you of Himself first, and all these things will be added unto you. Do not look at what others have and focus on getting a relationship with God. Do not want what they have; only want what God has for you. Ask God to show you what He has for you and find out what you have to do in order to get what He has. You will first have to go through much suffering and being without. If you do not want to be without, then you will lose out in the end. In order for you to become great, you first will have to go through and be without some things.

1. You will have to be without money.
2. You will have to go without honey (a man or a woman).
3. You will have to be without food.
4. You will have to be without clothes.
5. You will even have to be without a place to live.
6. You may even have to go without a car.

Are you willing to be without in order to gain? If you do not want to be without these things then you will not have what God has designed and intended for you to have and to be.

You may have to go through so much more before God can entrust you with the things that you really want. All God wants is you, and you will know when you're there if and when you stop wanting all the material things that other people have.

Matthew 6:33 states: *But seek (aim and strive after) first of all His kingdom and His righteousness (His way of doing and being right), and then all these things taken together will be given you besides.*

You have to prioritize what it is that you are doing. Seek Him in all that you do. You must always seek God first. You must seek Him early. You must seek Him every day. You must seek Him earnestly; and you must always seek Him faithfully. If you look to and acknowledge God, He will see about your business. Do not take the short cut; it just won't last. I have seen too many people overdoing it because they know that the more they work the more money, fame, and fortune they will receive. They end up doing things that cause their ministry to fall. Be extra careful about the reason why you come into the ministry.

It is God's work you're playing with. He will bring you down if you're doing it for the wrong reasons. Just like the anointing does not come overnight, it is the same way that fortune and fame do not come overnight. You have to focus yourself on God and He will make it happen all in due time. Take the time to love God first. He will bless you eventually and give you more than you ever dream possible. Focus on knowing the word; and God will put you out there when the right time comes. Do not force it to happen because a forced-ripe mango is sour and that's how your forced-ripe ministry will end up and you would have to start all over again. If you wait on God, He will ripen your ministry and cause you to bring forth good fruit even one hundred fold. He will also redeem the time that you've lost. Don't worry about how somebody else's ministry has taken off and yours is taking so long. You do not know the story behind why or how. It may simply be that they were under the fire longer than you have been or it could be that you still have some more lessons to learn that God is teaching. These are some lessons that you may have to go through.

1. You have to learn patience.
2. You have to learn self-control.
3. You have to learn to be a leader.
4. You have to learn to be humble.
5. You have to learn how to be a good Steward.
   a. With your money.
   b. With your time.
   c. With your things.

You should never be in too much of a rush to come out of the fire because you will be under-cooked and will have to go back in again. You do not want that because it will take even longer when you come out and have to go back in. Check yourself against these things and see if this speaks to you. You need to be honest with yourself and if needs be, to rethink your position. It's only then that God can help you.

You should always choose peace within yourself knowing that it was God who placed you there. No one would be able to remove you once God puts you in place. Do not want to be or even end up dying a copy of someone when God has made and formed you as an original. You are unique and have your own unique gifts that God has gifted you. Take the time to find out what those gifts are. Walk in your first calling. By this you will know your rightful ministry and will be compensated.

BEING ACCEPTED

Sometimes we want so badly to be accepted, or because we cannot say no, we end up taking positions thinking we can handle it.

Then we start the work only to find that it's too much for us, and we become too afraid or ashamed that we have hung our hats where our hands could not reach; and we stretch ourselves to the point that we pull a muscle. Now that we've taken the task or tasks, we feel stuck with no way out. However, there is always a way out. You just don't want to get out because it might be a prestigious position. We like to be "in-charge" and we like the feelings of importance, but that's no way to live. God wants us to be in the field that He has called us to be. It disappoints and displeases Him to see us in something other than what He's called us to do. Your life would work much better if you do only what God says. He knows what you can and cannot handle. Don't be jealous of someone who's doing something greater than you. How can a glass full be envious of a tub full, or how can a river that's full be envious of an ocean full. You cannot add more water to any of these things that's full. As my Bishop, Noel Jones likes to say, "If you're full, you're just full."

All these things get us frustrated and we stop bearing fruit. We say to God, "Well, God, You're the One that put me here. Now why is this happening to me?" Now you do not want to do it anymore. If you are at that point in your life then make sure; see if God was the one to put you there or was it you in and of yourself. These things do not only cause frustration, they also cause you to give up, even backslide. Before you do a job or a project,

1. Make sure God said it.
2. Make sure you're not forcing yourself to take on an assignment.
3. Make sure you give it up if it's taking a toll on you.
4. Make sure you are happy and at peace with what you are doing.

When you over work you may get sick and tired. You may get mean and nasty, you may get easily agitated, you may get easily frustrated, you may give up and you may even backslide. So do not do the things that God has not called you to do, but only what He has called you to do. You'll see that your life will be much easier.

2 Peter 2:20-22 states:

> *For if after they have escaped the pollutions of the world through [the full, personal] knowledge of our Lord and Savior Jesus Christ, they again become entangled in them and are overcome, their last condition is worse [for them] than the first. For never to have obtained a [full, personal] knowledge of the way of righteousness would have been better for them than, having obtained [such knowledge], to turn back from the holy commandment which was [verbally] delivered to them. There has befallen them the thing spoken of in the true proverb, the dog turns back to his own vomit, and the sow is washed only to wallow again in the mire.*

When you turn away from God, you will end up doing and being what the enemy wants and not what God wants.

1. You again become entangled.
2. Your last condition is worse than the first.
3. It's better if you have not obtained any knowledge of God.
4. It's worse to turn back from righteousness.

It would have been better if you did not accept God in the first place than to have known Him and turn from Him. That is what the enemy strives for. The devil loves to get those people to make a fool of them. When you have been a Christian and you have backslidden, this is what you're really doing. You were at one time clean. However, now you are back to your old ways and that is what the devil wants. He wants us to give up on God. Giving up on God is the worse thing that an individual can ever do. When we give up, we lose out on our own destiny and worse, maybe even heaven. Don't give up a chance to spend eternity with the Creator who is our Father.

> *I know your industry and activities, laborious toil and trouble, and your patient endurance, and how you cannot tolerate wicked [men] and have tested and critically appraised those who call [themselves] apostles (special messengers of Christ) and yet are not, and have found them to be impostors and liars. I know you are enduring patiently and are bearing up for My name's sake, and you have not fainted or become exhausted or grown weary. But I have this [one charge to make] against you: that you have left (abandoned) the love that you had at first [you have deserted Me, your first love]. (Revelation 2:2-4)*

Don't let being in the wrong position stop you from your life with Christ. You can be working so hard that you forget to spend time in prayer and lose the love you once had for God. You need to remember the zeal you once had and rekindle it. Do not keep slipping away and think that nothing is wrong. Refocus your life to God and He will help you and draw you closer to Him. He will not fail you nor will He forsake you if you do not give up on Him.

We all need to get into the right position and see not only how much better you will feel, but also how much better your life would be. Ask God, what your position is. Ask God where He wants you to be. Acknowledge Him in all things and watch Him bring about what it is that He has for you. In all things, consult God and He will direct your path.

CHAPTER 20
THE JUDGMENTS OF GOD

The judgment of God comes by us not obeying the things that God had said. He has placed four kinds of judgment. We need to try and straighten out our lives before He brings wrath upon the earth and destroy all mankind.

The four judgments of God that we have to face are:

1. The judgment of sin.
2. The judgment seat of Christ (Christians are judged).
3. The white-throne judgment (for sinners and angels).
4. The judgment of reward.

WHAT IS JUDGMENT?

Judgment is the ability to make considered decisions or form sensible opinions. The judgment of men: God has said that we should judge ourselves according to His word. Among God's covenant people, judgment is based on His revelation and instruction that He had given to us. We must always be able to distinguish between right and wrong. Before you judge:

1. You must have an understanding mind.
2. You must be able to discern between good and bad.
3. You must not take sides because you like one over the other.
4. You must check yourself to make sure that you're not biased.

1 Kings 3:9 states: *So give your servant an understanding mind and a hearing heart to judge your people that I may discern between good and bad. For who is able to judge and rule this your great people?*

God has placed people, as you can see, to rule over us and that can rightly judge a situation and give justice like what Solomon did. He was wise and was able to judge correctly whose the living baby was.

1 Kings 3:16-28 states:

Then two women who had become mothers out of wedlock came and stood before the king. And the woman said, O my lord, I and this woman dwell in one house; and I was delivered of a child with her in the house. And the third day after I was delivered, this woman also was delivered. And we were together; no stranger was with us, just we two in the house. And this woman's child died in the night because she lay on him. And she arose at midnight and took my son from beside me while your handmaid slept and laid him in her bosom and laid her dead child in my bosom. And when I rose to nurse my child, behold, he was dead. But when I had considered him in the morning, behold, it was not the son I had borne. But the other woman said, No! But the living one is my son, and the dead one is your son! And this one said, No! But the dead son is your son, and the living is my son. Thus they spoke before the king. The king said, one says, this is my son that is alive and yours is the dead one. The other woman says, No! But your son is the dead one and mine is the living one. And the king said, Bring me a sword. And they brought a sword to the king. And the king said, Divide the living child in two and give half to the one and half to the other. Then the mother of the living child said to the king, for she yearned over her son, O my lord, give her the living baby, and by no means slay him. But the other said, Let it not be mine or yours, but divide him. Then the king said, Give her [who pleads for his life] the living baby, and by no means slay him. She is the child's mother. And all Israel heard of the judgment, which the king had made, and they stood in awe of him, for they saw that the wisdom of God was in him to do justice.

God has put our jurisdiction system in place to help us to rule out good from bad so that the bad must be punished. When you judge you must take these into consideration.

1. Consider and do what is right.
2. Consider and help the widow.
3. Consider and help the fatherless.
4. Consider and seek out proper justice.
5. Consider and help those that are oppressed.

When you do these things God will in turn bless you and give you more to do because you judge correctly.

Isaiah 1:17 states: *Learn to do right! Seek justice, relieve the oppressed, and correct the oppressor. Defend the fatherless, plead for the widow.*

The Lord wants to have mercy upon us. That's why he waits patiently and reminds us of His word so that we can in our selves correct the wrong that we have done and make it right. We need to seek Him daily and delight in His ways and not forsake the ordinances then judgment would not come to us. God hates sin. He does not want us to judge anyone because it will cause you to fail. God hates when we sin and judging incorrectly is a sin.

1. God hates when you falsely accuse people.
2. God hates when you have hate in your heart.
3. God hates when you conspire against another.
4. God hates when you think that you're better than another.

Do not let God be displeased with you for judging incorrectly. He will not let it go until justice is served.

Zechariah 8:16-17 states:

> *These are the things that you shall do: speak every man the truth with his neighbor; render the truth and pronounce the judgment or verdict that makes for peace in [the courts at] your gates. And let none of you think or imagine or devise evil or injury in your hearts against his neighbor, and love no false oath, for all these things I hate, says the Lord.*

We should know by now the things that the Lord hates. We need to stay away from them or He will bring judgment down on us very quickly. The Lord said that the meek He will guide in judgment and the meek will He teach His way, according to Psalms 25:9. So we aught always to treat our neighbors right and God would have no reason to judge us.

WHY WOULD GOD JUDGE US?

> *Do not judge and criticize and condemn others, so that you may not be judged and criticized and condemned yourselves. For just as you judge and criticize and condemn others, you will be judged and criticized and condemned, and in accordance with the measure you [use to] deal out to others, it will be dealt out again to you. (Mat. 7:1-2)*

God loves us. He does not want us to be harmed in anyway. However, like your own children that have done wrong where you have to punish them, the same it is with God. The difference is; God punishes us in ways He knows will get us to stop doing the things that we do. With our children, we may take away their favorite toys, or games, or even beat them, but sometimes that doesn't even faze them. Some of us will be punished with few stripes and some with many stripes according to the degree of our responsibilities and the seriousness of our sins.

God will bring judgment very quickly upon us,

1. If we judge others wrongfully.
2. If we judge others without a cause.
3. If we judge others that are in need.
4. If we overlook those who are oppressing others.
5. If we tell others not to do certain things and we end up doing them ourselves.

When you make judgment on those that God says not to, then not only are you being disobedient; you are also causing your own self to be judged. You are causing your own self to be punished by God Himself when you make judgment on those that God says not to.

Romans 2:2-6 states:

> *[But] we know that the judgment (adverse verdict, sentence) of God falls justly and in accordance with truth upon those who practice such things. And do you think or imagine, o man, when you judge and condemn those who practice such things and yet do them yourself, that you will escape God's judgment and elude His sentence and adverse verdict? Or are you [so blind as to] trifle with and presume upon and despised and underestimate the wealth of His kindness and forbearance and long-suffering patience? Are you unmindful or actually ignorant [of the fact] that God's kindness is intended to lead you to repent (to change your mind and inner man to accept God's will)? But by your callous stubbornness and impenitence of heart you are storing up wrath and indignation for yourself on the day of wrath and indignation, when God's righteous judgment (just doom) will be revealed. For He will render to every man according to his works [justly, as his deeds deserve].*

God holds us responsible for His people that He has entrusted to us. We must be very careful with them. We are held accountable,

1. If we have stubbornness towards another.
2. If we are impatient with those that He has entrusted to us.
3. If we store up wrath and hatred against another.
4. If we have anger and malice one to another.

Therefore you have no excuse or defense or justification, O man, whoever you are who judges and condemns another. For in posing as judge and passing sentence on another, you condemn yourself, because you who judge are habitually practicing the very same things [that you censure and denounce]. (Romans 2:1)

God judges those who will not do His will. He is a loving and forgiving God, but He would not wait forever to get you straightened out. He will send His people to speak with you and will give you many chances. You do not live forever, and one day your time will run out where it might be too late.

THE JUDGMENT SEAT OF CHRIST

When we as Christians die, we will all have to give an account for the things we did on earth. We have to come before God's face and tell Him what and why we did or did not do the things we were told to do. The fire from His eyes will try every man's work whether is good or bad. If your works are built on gold, silver, cars, houses, and lands, these things shall be burned up. However, you shall be saved once your heart is right with God. If it's built on meanness, hatred, bitterness, and unforgiveness, you shall be burnt in the lake of fire. What is not good shall be burnt, but what is good shall remain. God will do and say the things that He has promised before the foundation of the world.

1. We will appear before Him.
2. We will be asked some questions.
3. We will be placed on either His right or left according to what we have done.
4. We will have our lives flash before us to see our behaviors while we were yet living.
5. We will be sentenced to eternal punishment if bad and to eternal life if good.

We will see all the things that we did when we were on earth whether it's good or bad and depending on what we've done God will judge accordingly.

2 Corinthians 5:10 states:

> For we must all appear and be revealed as we are before the judgment seat of Christ, so that each one may receive [his pay] according to what he has done in the body. Whether good or evil [considering what his purpose and motive have been, and what he has achieved, been busy with, and given himself and his attention to accomplishing].

We will be receiving each a reward for what we have done. He will ask us to give an account.

Luke 12:47-48 states:

> And that servant who knew his master's will but did not get ready or act as he would wish him to act shall be beaten with many [lashes]. But he who did not know and did things worthy of a beating shall be beaten with few [lashes]. For everyone to whom much is given, of him shall much be required; and

of him to whom men entrust much, they will require and demand all the more.

Do not think that because you did not know, you would be excused. There's no escaping this judgment. It is going to happen, just as you know that one-day you will die. Stop fooling yourself and make your life right with God. There are questions that God will ask.

1. What have you done for the poor?
2. Did you visit those that are bound and in prison?
3. Did you help the widowed?
4. Did you feed the hungry?
5. Did you reach out to the little children, or did you cast them away?

These are questions that He will ask, and what are you going to tell Him? There are no excuses that will make you escape the judgment and get you into heaven. You have to know what you're about now before it's too late. Tomorrow is not promised to any man. So do the right thing today while you still have time. These are things that you would try to do.

1. You would try to lie to Him.
2. You would try to bribe Him.
3. You would try reasoning with Him.
4. You would even try to make promises to Him.

All this would be too late. Don't let it happen to you. God loves you. He is coming to you again telling you to get your life right. He is coming soon and He wants you to be ready.

Revelation 3:21 states: *He who overcome (is victorious). I will grant him to sit beside Me on My throne, as I Myself overcame (was victorious) and sat down beside My Father on His throne.*

If we are good, we will be rewarded and be able to be with Him and do things with Him. We get to sit beside Him. We get to have communion with Him. We get to have fellowship with Him. We get to dine with Him. We also get to worship and sing melodies of praise to Him. We have to start now to make sure we are living the life that He wants us to live. Would you make it in? Only those who endure to the end and stick it out will make it. Would you be one who makes it in, or would you be left out?

Joel 1:15 states: *Alas for the day! For the day of [the judgment of] the Lord is at hand, and as a destructive tempest from the Almighty will it come.*

It is only a matter of time before this happens; and where would you spend eternity? God wants us to change our ways and acknowledge and serve Him fully. We will say that we have done many things in His name.

1. We will say that we have healed the sick.
2. We will say that we have cast out demons.
3. We will say that we have preached and many were saved.
4. We will say that we helped and give to the needy and to those that You have commanded us.

We will try to reason with God. We will be in tears trying to fix what we have done, but it will not be the correct time to do any of that. God will not be in any mood to hear your cries for forgiveness.

Matthew 7:22-23 states:

> *Many will say to me on that day, Lord, Lord, have we not prophesied in Your name and driven out demons in Your name and done many mighty works in Your name? And then I will*

say to them openly (publicly), I never knew you; depart from
Me you who act wickedly [disregarding My commands].

We all have been saved at one time or another. We have also backslidden at one time or another, but there comes a time when we have to make a decision to follow Christ and to do what's right in the sight of the Lord. Although we have done many miraculous things like heal the sick, cast out evil spirits, raised the dead, caused the blind to see, the deaf to hear and so on, but if we do not live right we still would end up in hell.

Doing right will not get you in heaven. It takes more than that. It's by us doing, obeying, and keeping His commandments, praying, reading your word, spending time with Him and forming a relationship with Him is what will get you into heaven. When we do get that relationship with Him, we then will need to be and do what He says. If we do not, we may hear Him say.

1. We need to have had compassion.
2. We need to have had forgiveness.
3. We need to have had understanding.
4. We need to have shown love.

If we would do these things, we would be confident that God would show us mercy on the Day of Judgment.

1 John 4:17 states:

In this [union and communion with Him] love is brought
to completion and attains perfection with us, that we may
have confidence for the day of judgment [with assurance and
boldness to face Him], because as He is, so are we in this
world.

If we love Him, we will spend eternity with Him. His words declare that all we have to do is live right. Live the way He wants us to live. It could and will be hard at times but nothing good comes easy, so strive to enter into the straight and narrow gate because it leads you to life.

THE WHITE THRONE JUDGMENT

The white throne judgment is where the sinners and angels including Satan will be judged. It is called the great judgment day. Christians will also be participating in this judgment. Christians will be judging the angels. We will get a chance to pay back Satan and all his imps for what they did to us while we were on earth. God will also judge those that are not His. He will cast all those people along with Satan and his angels who were cast out of heaven to hell.

For if God spared not the angels that sinned, but cast them down to hell, and delivered them into chains of darkness, to be reserved unto judgment. (2Peter 2:4 KJV)

And the angels, which kept not their first estate, but left their own habitation, he hath reserved in everlasting chains under darkness unto the judgment of the great day. (Jude 6 KJV)

The sea will also give up the dead, and they will be judged according to their works. Every thing that you have done whether good or bad shall be judged. This is a sad and dreadful day for those who chose not to believe on the Lord Jesus Christ. Some of you may think that you were good enough to get to heaven.

1. You will think that because you donate your time and money that God will accept you.

2. You will think that because you build a church for your pastor that God will accept you.
3. You will think that because you visit the sick and shut-in that you have done enough and God will accept you.
4. You will think that because you have given to the poor and to the homeless that you have done your duty and God will accept you.
5. You will think that because you went to church on Easter, thanksgiving, Christmas, and New Years that you have made your quota when it comes to church and that God will accept you.

These are things that will also be in the book because everything that you do will be recorded and God will show you everything that you have done. Many of you will be shocked on that day because you are fooling yourself while you're still here on earth. Know the truth. Learn what it takes for you to have your name written in the Lamb's Book of Life before it's too late. God is merciful; however, in that day He will not be so merciful towards those who rejected His precious Son, Jesus. He's done too much for you to have you go to hell because of ignorance. He's giving you many chances while you're yet alive to repent, to love and to serve Him so you can live with Him at that great day.

And I saw a great white throne, and him that sat on it, from whose face the earth and the heaven fled away; and there was found no place for them. And I saw the dead, small and great, stand before God; and the books were opened: and another book was opened, which is the book of life: and the dead were judged out of those things which were written in the books, according to their works. And the sea gives up the dead, which were in it; and death and hell delivered up the dead, which were in them: and they were judge every man according to their works. And death and hell were cast into the lake of fire. This is the second death. And who sever was not found in the book of life was cast into the lake of fire. (Revelation 20:11-15 KJV)

When you die and you are not saved (that is you did not accept Jesus in your heart and live the God kind of life) you will go straight to hell. When the end of time comes then you will be released from hell to be judged by God. If you are still living when Jesus comes back then you will appear before God. He will look in the Book of Life for your name, and if it is not found therein then you will be cast into hell also.

JUDGMENTS AND REWARDS

God is a God not only of judgment, He is also a rewarder of those who just not only seek Him, but He is also a rewarder of those who give all that they have for Him. God does not want what we have. He just wants to see if we are willing to give up the little that we do have to Him and for Him. When you've made up in your mind to follow Him, He will put you to the test to see how much you love Him. Do you love Him? Will you give up what you have for Him? That will be the test to see if you really mean it when you say, "I love You Lord." Here are some things you might and or will be asked to give up.

1. You will or could be asked to give up your house.
2. You will or could be asked to give up all your money.
3. You will or could be asked to give up your friends.
4. You will or could be asked to leave your children.
5. You will or could be asked to leave your family,
   a. Such as your cousins.
   b. Such as your uncles and aunts.
   c. Such as your brothers and sisters.
   d. Such as your mother and father
   e. Such as your spouse.

6. You will or could be asked to isolate yourself for a season.

There is no telling what God might want you to give up for Him. Remember, He's no respecter of persons. So if He's asked one person, He will also ask another which might very well be you.

Matthew 16:27 states: *For the Son of Man is going to come in glory (majesty, splendor) of His Father with His angels, and then he will render account and reward every man in accordance with what he has done.*

The Lord will check to see what we've done and will reward us for our faithfulness. God is a just God and He will never let us go without if we remain faithful. He is faithful that promised. We can rest assured that we will get our due reward all at the appointed and due time in our lives.

We all shall be rewarded—to every man according to what he or she did on earth. It is important to give to others and always lend a helping hand whenever you can and whenever it is needed. But this will not hold up on judgment day if your heart with which you were doing it was not right, or if you did not accept Jesus as Lord and Savior of your life. All that you would have done would be in vain for not having a relationship with Christ. All your giving, lending, helping, and serving would go to waste and would all be for nothing because you will still be placed on His left side and end up in eternal damnation.

1. All because you did not stop to pray everyday.
2. All because you did not take the time to build a relationship with Him.
3. All because you did not take the time out to find out who He really was.

4. All because you did not want to read your bible and learn what and why He came to earth.

Do not let our being too busy keep us from spending time getting to know God. It will be our downfall if we do.

Matthew 19:27-29 states:

> *Then Peter answered Him, saying, behold we have left [our] all and have become Your disciples [sided with Your party and followed you]. What then shall we receive? Jesus said to them, truly I say to you, in the new age [the Messianic rebirth of the world], when the son of man shall sit down on the throne of His glory, you who have [become My disciples, side with My party and] followed Me will also sit on twelve thrones and judge the twelve tribes of Israel. And anyone and everyone who has left houses, or brothers, or sisters, or father, or mother, or children, or lands for My name's sake will receive many [even a hundred] times more and will inherit eternal life.*

Since we have left our all to follow Christ, He will give us back and even more of what we have given up. We can never outgive God. If He's asking us to give it up, it just simply means that He has much more to give us after we've suffered a while. If you are faithful, you will receive a crown.

There are four crowns.

1. The crown of righteousness

2 Timothy 4:8 states:

> *[As to what remains] henceforth there is laid up for me the [victor's] crown of righteousness [for being right with God*

and doing right], which the Lord, the righteous judge, will award to me and recompense me on that [great] day-and not to me only, but also to all those who have loved and yearned for and welcomed His appearing (his return).

2. The crown of glory.

1 Peter 5:4 states: *And [then] when the Chief Shepherd is revealed, you will win the conqueror's crown of glory.*

3. The incorruptible crown.

In 1 Corinthians 9:25 states: *And every man that striveth for the mastery is temperate in all things. Now they do it to obtain a corruptible crown, but we an incorruptible.* (KJV)

4. The crown of life.

James 1:12 states:

Blessed (happy, to be envied) is the man who is patient under trial and stands up under temptation, for when he has stood the test and been approved, he will receive [the victor's] crown of life which God has promised to those who love Him.

Revelation 2:10 states:

Fear nothing that you are about to suffer. [Dismiss your dread and your fears!] Behold the devil is indeed about to throw some of you into prison, that you may be tested and proved and critically appraised, and for ten days you will have affliction. Be loyally faithful unto death [even if you must die for it], and I will give you the crown of life

If you love God and serve Him, you will receive a crown. It is a promise and God always keeps His word.

God rewards faithfulness. He watches to see what we will do with the little that He has entrusted to us. If we do what we're supposed to do, then He will reward us by giving us much more responsibility. This would indicate how pleased He is with us and He will willingly give us more.

The Individual Prayer

Father in the name of Your precious Son, Jesus, I come to You with my hands lifted up sundering my all to You. Please forgive me all my sins and help me to live for You. You are my life and I want to be like Your precious Son Jesus. Help me to be holy for You. Help me to be pleasing to You. I give my all to You because You are worthy. You are God and God alone, and there is none like You. I love You and I know that I have many things that I need to overcome. Please help me to overcome all my adversities. Help me to birth out the things that You said I am. Please help me to let go of everyone that has hurt me. I thank You for everything that You've done for me. I am Yours and Yours alone. Thank You for being there for me even if I cannot trace You. I thank You for all that You've done, are doing, and will do in my life. In Jesus name Amen.

Lord I Surrender

Lord I surrender my life to You
I want to be just like You
You are my life and heart
If I don't have You I'll fall apart
You are the One that I adore
You are the One that I implore
You are the One I waited for
You are the One I want and no more
You are the One for me
You make me complete
No matter what I've done
No matter where I've been
You are always there for me
Lord I give my life to You
Lord I give my heart to You
Lord I give my mind to You
Lord I will give You anything
You are all I dreamed about
You are all I ever wanted
In my life and in my heart

A Prayer for You

Holy Father I come to You today standing in the gap for all my brothers and my sisters that are in need. Father they have gone through and are going through so much. Please help them to know that You are there, that You love them and that You have not forgotten them. Father, help them to know that You have not left them to go through by themselves. My Holy Father, I thank You for who You are and for how much You love Your people. Father please heal Your people from all their childhood pains. Help them to forgive the ones that have hurt them so that they can move on with their lives. Father there's nothing too hard for You to do and I'm asking You to please reach down and bring total and complete healing in their body, mind, heart, soul and spirit. Father, please bring physical, emotional, financial, and spiritual healing to Your people. Father please take unforgiveness, hatred, jealousy, envy, and everything that is not like You away from them. Father, please show up and show out in their lives. Every sickness, every disease, every infirmity, I curse you in the name of Jesus; and I command you to go back into the pit of hell where you belong. Satan, the Lord rebukes you. I thank You Holy Father that You hear me always. Have Your way in Your people's lives. In Jesus mighty and precious name, Amen.

You May Be Going Through

You may be going through right now
But you would not be there for long
You may be going through right now
But you would come out strong
You may be going through right now
But God is always near to you
You may be going through right now
But He knows all your struggles
You may be going through right now
But you shall soon give God all the praise
You may be going through right now
But you will soon feel light and free
You may be going through right now
But God will always make a way
You may be going through right now
But God will bring you out
Without a shadow of a doubt

A SINNER'S PRAYER

Father, I come to You a sinner. Please come into my heart and forgive me of all my sins. I believe that Your Son Jesus died, shed His blood for me, and rose again from the grave on the third day so that I can live. Wash me in Your precious blood and make me as white as snow. I renounce Satan and put him under my feet. Make me a new creature and write my name in the Lamb's Book of Life. I thank You for loving me. In Jesus name, Amen.

NOTES

NOTES

NOTES